BRICK
20

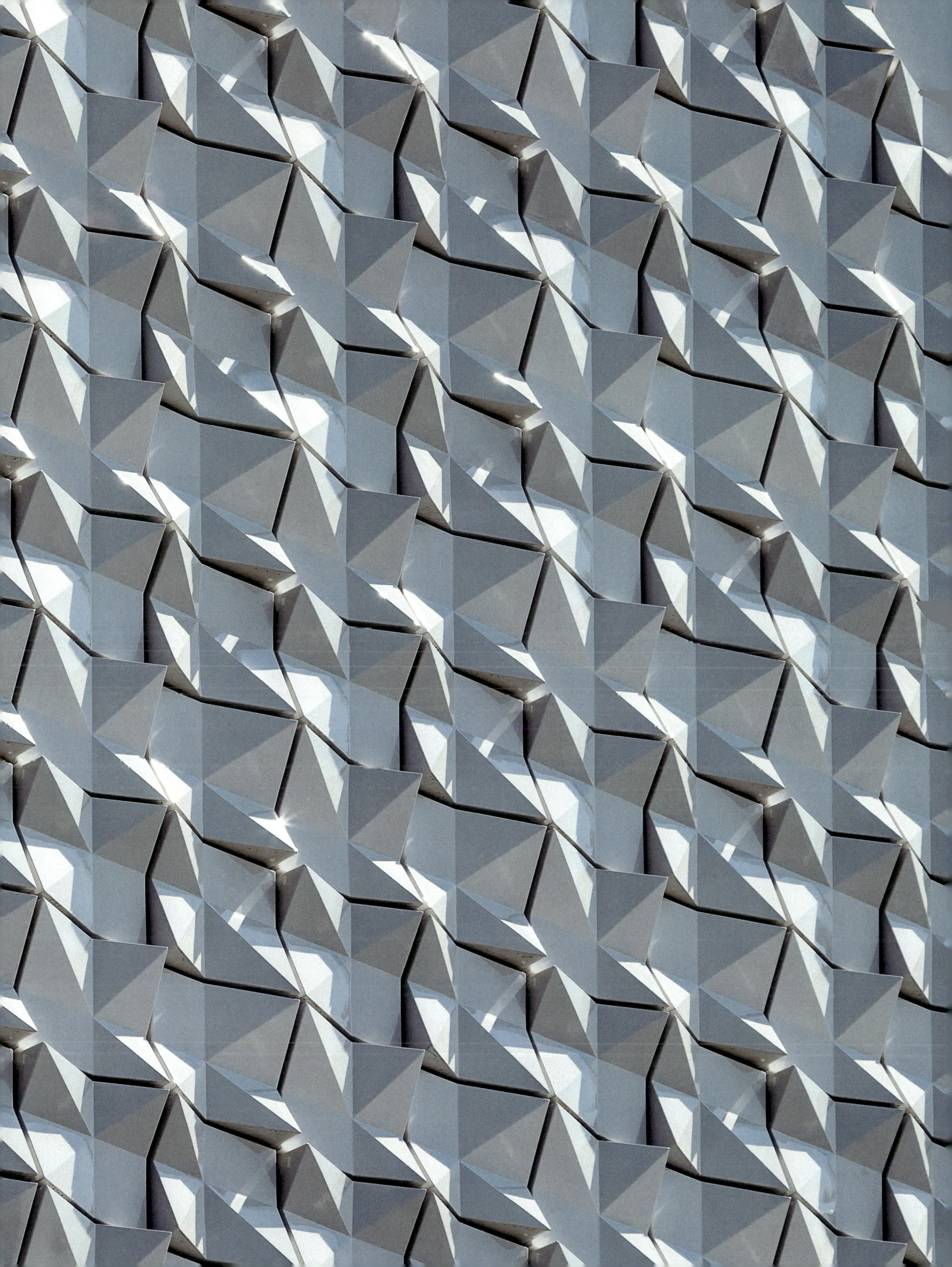

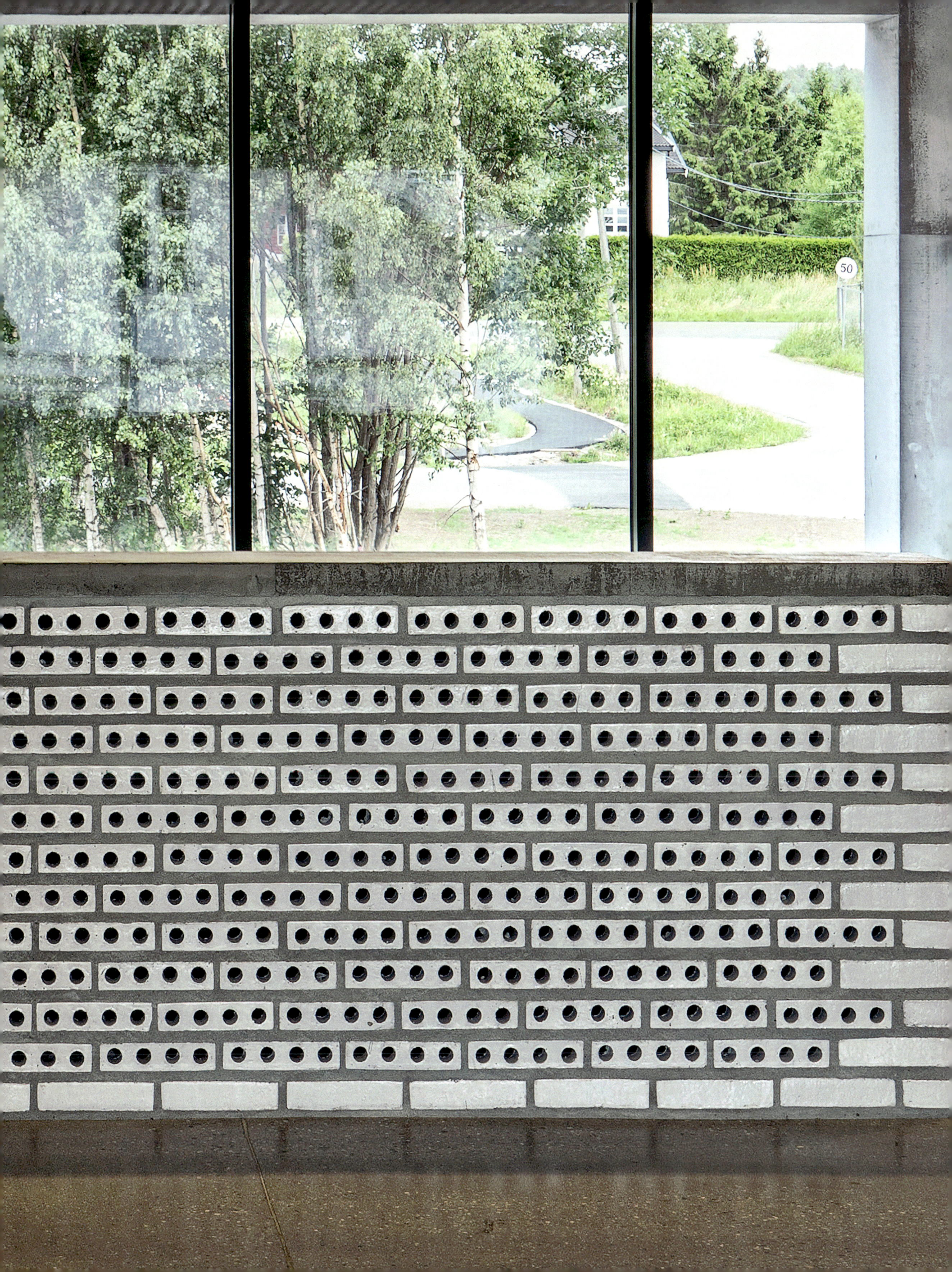
50

"Clay is simply an elementary material—
and always good for innovation
in technology, function and design."
Hubertus Adam

BRICK 20

PARK BOOKS

wienerberger

BRICK 20

Feeling at home

Living together

Working together

Sharing public spaces

Building outside the box

The jury: Tina Gregorič, Mette Kynne Frandsen, Toni Gironès Saderra, Jonathan Sergison and Helena Glantz

The Competition

The Brick Award offers architects from all over the world the opportunity to introduce contemporary, innovative brick architecture and make it known to a broad public. The aim is to inspire, to put design concepts up to discussion and to search for new ways to implement architectural ideas—with the help of ceramic materials.

In 2020, Wienerberger is awarding this internationally established prize for the ninth time. 644 projects from 55 countries were submitted. In the first phase of the two-stage selection process, a panel of architecture journalists nominated 50 projects from all of the submissions. The composition of this committee—as well as the perspective in the evaluation of the projects—changes with each Brick Award. Anneke Bokern, Jonathan Glancey and Christian Holl, who also wrote the project texts in the book, served on this panel for the Brick Award 20. The selection criteria remained unchanged: the use of ceramic building materials, the degree of innovation, sustainability throughout the construction process, the architectural quality of the project and the adequacy, introduced by the preliminary jury as an additional point at the last Brick Award, are crucial for a nomination. In this connection, the latter means that the project should also be judged on its purpose, the type of building and the cultural context. Therefore, the assessment of a social construction project, for instance, takes into account the limited budget resources.

Content-related tendencies, which are also reflected in the nominations selected by the preliminary jury, can be gathered from the large number of submissions: One area concerns the use of bricks in the urban context. The closing of gap sites, the expansion of existing buildings and additions within smaller-scale settlement structures are recurring construction tasks that show the high "integration ability" of the material.

A further focus of this year's submissions is on social or prototypical projects. Knowledge transfer, self-construction and the possibility of using an easily producible material available almost everywhere are at the forefront here. In both cases, the structural-physical properties and recyclability of bricks play a major role.

From a design point of view, there is a trend towards fired red brick, which is used in specific formats and with different additives to perfectly match the particular structure.

In the second phase, the winners of the competition were determined by a jury of international architects, whose members this year were Mette Kynne Frandsen (Denmark), Helena Glantz (Sweden), Tina Gregorič (Slovenia), Toni Gironès Saderra (Spain) and Jonathan Sergison (United Kingdom). In the course of the jury meeting in Vienna, they emphasized the wide geographical and content-related range of the nominations, the quality of planning and implementation, as well as the variety of design and the juxtaposition of tradition and innovation. The amount of the prize-worthy buildings was so high that six instead of five winners were ultimately chosen and an additional four honorary mentions awarded.

This book presents the 50 nominees, including the winning projects of the Brick Award 20. Each structure is documented with texts, photographs and plan material. Moreover, the winning projects will also be featured in short videos that can be found at www.brickaward.com.

Dear friends of architecture, we wish you a lot of pleasure discovering the brick architecture masterpieces of the Brick Award 20!

"The focus of our actions is the human human being."

Heimo Scheuch
CEO Wienerberger

OUR MISSION

We create affordable and sustainable living space. We assume responsibility for the generations to come.

Editorial

Dear friends of fine architecture,

Exquisite constructed beauty captures the eye at the very first glance. It draws the gaze from one detail to the next, up the façade to the roof and then down to the base, arousing a desire to learn more about the concept envisaged by the architect. At the same time, a building reveals a great deal about how it is used, those who live in it and the architects who designed it.

In cities too, subtle architectural details give very clear indications of the major challenges of our day. Key issues such as climate change, diminishing resources, global population growth, increasing urbanization, affordable housing, changing patterns of mobility and work as well as the rapid advance of digitalization in all areas of life exert a significant influence on town planning, urban architecture and infrastructure.

As a technology and innovation leader in the construction sector, Wienerberger recognizes its role and indeed obligation with regard to making substantial contributions to overcoming current global challenges, with a view to shaping future-proof and healthy living environments on a sustainable basis. Architects play a vital part in meeting this need.

Wienerberger has a long and proud tradition of sustainability: Our sustainability concept encompasses three dimensions – ecological, environmental and social –, all of which play an essential role in every measure and product. Two hundred years ago, Wienerberger began to manufacture building materials that enable the construction of sustainable, durable buildings and affordable housing.

Many of these buildings have become part of our architectural heritage and many still play an important role in meeting the demand for architecture today. The popularity of this construction material that has been used for thousands of years is unbroken. Bricks and the use of innovative, efficient system solutions still safeguard the wealth of opportunities afforded to subsequent generations and the active contribution made to environmental protection. In addition, the durability and versatility of the diverse ceramic construction materials combined with their timelessly classic, yet contemporary look offer architects so many different and innovative ways to use them, enabling exciting and aesthetic solutions.

It is particularly important for us to ask these outstanding architects to step into the spotlight so we can celebrate them. It is with pride that we acknowledge the high quality of the brick architecture projects from all over the world that were submitted for the Ninth Brick Award. We would like to thank the international jury of architects who selected the winners of the Brick Award for the valuable contribution they made in the selection process and of course all the architects.

We hope that as connoisseurs of fine architecture you will enjoy reading this BRICK 20 Book and find inspiration and pleasure as you discover these remarkable architectural projects.

Heimo Scheuch
CEO Wienerberger AG

Feeling at home

Living together

Working together

Sharing public spaces

Building outside the box

Feeling at home

JOB FLORIS

Exploring Authenticities Towards Thicker and Thinner

Job Floris

While reflecting on the role of the brick in the current era, a couple of observations come into mind—concerning the current treatment of masonry and challenges for the near future.

Over the past decades, one can determine a group of materials that have surrounded us abundantly, since they are to be found in a great amount of built structures. This group of "survivors" could be considered very sustainable in regard to their presence. These materials belong to the basic core materials: being around for many years and having proven to be useful in a wide variety of applications. Moreover, these materials have shown to be flexible and transformable in form and appearance. Their reinvention and rediscovery were made possible by many generations, a quality which makes them survive; think of stone, concrete, wood, steel. And think of brick.

Most of the members of this group have the ability to operate as construction and as cladding; as plates and as beams and columns, which largely determines their success. Their functionality and validity in society are inextricably linked with the economic climate of an era. During Chicago's big building boom in the 1880s, for example, the inventive use of steel gradually made this construction material more favorable, since it allowed the building process to speed up, despite the brick structures—which required more time to erect. On numerous occasions in history, changes in the preferred material have taken place. Sometimes they were driven by speed, sometimes by the available material handling knowledge.

Obviously, among this group of primal materials the presence of masonry—or, more specifically, the brick—has remained, due its rather direct and simple method of production. The manual craft involved caused the brick to have this specific quality: the small grain. For architects, these fine dimensions increase adaptivity towards a high level of the freedom of form. Louis Kahn's National Assembly building in Dhaka, for instance, is among the clearest explorations of this specific quality of brick. Recently, the "House of Memory" by the Milanese office baukuh has also demonstrated that the brick is able to act as a contemporary pixel and function as a remarkable carrier of memories and traditions. Yet, in recent decades, for some architects the brick seems to have slightly lost attractivity, being unjustifiably disqualified as a type of "romantic, conservative type of cladding" with the sole functionality of providing a shield against rain and moisture. From the economic and building physics perspectives, this role could be played by other, more efficient materials as well.

"Brick is a type of material we are able to relate to."

However, there are several proper arguments to value the continuity of bricks. Caused by arguments which might be less measurable and rational, but more sensitive and phenomenological of nature instead. For one, because this is a type of material we are able to relate to: the origins and substance are understandable, and used to be even stronger. The soil—on which life took place—was heated and stacked for reasons of protection. Therefore, it strongly resonates to the idea of accommodation and protection. Together with the idea of being touched by the hand, these aspects provide a character of authenticity.

Do these observations result in a stagnant situation of acceptance, a product that is complete and developed to its utmost optimum, with no undiscovered fields? Not at all. Although contrary, at least two challenges can be distinguished, both with their own validity and beauty, and both intriguing for further explorations.

Thicker

In recent years, the emergence of the brick as a loadbearing element has gradually been gaining ground. This requires a type of brick that is denser and larger dimensioned, in pace with the idea of robustness and weight. More important: it is reestablishing brick's status as a genuine loadbearing material—which brings us back to the future. Among the positive sides of this development is the idea of one singular material that is thorough and not subdivided into layers—and the absence of a plastic type of insulation. Besides the environmental advantage, the interior climate will benefit from this, too, as the material—thick as it is—will have the capacity to gradually breathe, thereby improving the quality of the dwelling place. At the same time, all the precious characteristics of the brick, such as the rich nuancing and the beauty of aging, will survive. As a result, the interior could have the same finishing as the exterior, since one and the same element is being used. For those architects, the paramount argument is being interested in a high level of authenticity, understood as not covered, nor further processed, and directly visible. One can speculate on how this direction would make the house appealing as a place of solidity and protection. This would reinforce the idea of the house as an object built once in a lifetime, there to stay for a long period, offering new family members, new generations, to make it part of their lives—something which rarely seems to happen in the Netherlands, Belgium, Luxembourg, Northern Germany etc., today.

Thinner

Simultaneously, the other direction might mean an acceptance with "less of the material brick." Since the process of industrialization and robotization has enabled more prefabrication, this might have brought the brick towards performing with more slenderness. In fact, a key characterization for this product would be to emphasize it as *ceramics* instead of *masonry*. Because in this field of play, the brick has become more of a slender tile, playing a most efficient role in keeping up appearances. When fully engaging with this material, it becomes more productive to consider the slender brick as a tile, releasing the object from the idea of mimicking a brick. This would also enable the practice of cladding prefab concrete panels with thin slips of brickwork to be transcended, allowing more freedom in forms and patterns without losing the rich nuancing of a ceramic material.

In this context, the recent work of the Genovese architect Francesca Torzo is worth mentioning. At the end of 2019, the Z33 museum in Hasselt, Belgium will open to the public, containing an impressively rich façade of ceramics. Although this cladding seems to perfectly blend in with the built environment, it is not necessary to provide a very precise name for this ambiguous product, bringing to mind both bricks and tiles.

Besides, the theme of cladding—a topic once introduced by Gottfried Semper—acting as a thin layer which can be applied, might perhaps also anticipate the idea of transformation and change. As the application effort might be less substantial and more affordable, it would facilitate the changing of appearances in relatively short periods. Considering the brick as rich tile might appeal to yet another type of authenticity.

TALLER | MAURICIO ROCHA + GABRIELA CARRILLO

Iturbide Studio

Mauricio Rocha and Gabriela Carrillo

PROJECT NAME
Iturbide Studio

ARCHITECT/S
Taller | Mauricio Rocha + Gabriela Carrillo, Mexico City / Mexico

BUILDING PURPOSE
Artist's studio

LOCATION
Mexico City, Mexico

CONSTRUCTION PERIOD
2014–2016

BRICK TYPE
Clay blocks, pavement clinkers

BRICK AWARD CATEGORY
Feeling at home

BRICK 20 Category Winner

Graciela Iturbide is a Mexican photographer, famous for black and white photographs of Mexican peasant women. In 1991, her son, Mauricio Rocha, who runs the Taller de Arquitectura together with Gabriela Carrillo, built a house for her in the historic Coyoacán district of Mexico City. More than twenty years later, his mother commissioned him with another building: Her studio was to be erected on an empty lot in the immediate vicinity of the house. Her only condition: it had to be made of brick.

The architects more than fulfilled this requirement. On the 7 × 14-meter plot, they built a three-story brick turret that rises out of the fabric of low-rise neighboring buildings. Exposed masonry is not uncommon in Mexico, but it has been taken to extremes in this building: Brick is omnipresent inside and out; its use seems almost obsessive.

Consisting of three stacked, 28-square-meter rooms, the structure is flanked on the north and south sides by a patio. All rooms open through wall-sized sliding windows to the two courtyards. On the ground floor there is a reception room, on the first floor a living room. The second floor houses the photo studio with the partly covered terrace above it. Stairways and ancillary spaces are hidden in a narrow, laterally arranged access core.

> "A work that above all sought silence, synthesis, continuous, repetitive and almost obsessive use of a single material."

All of the walls were made of reddish-brown, handmade bricks from a manufacturer in Puebla 150 kilometers away. One double row of flat, long bricks in an asymmetrical stretcher bond alternates with a series of twice as thick, standing bricks. While the walls of the building core are laid brick to brick, depending on the location and the desired incidence of light, a different number of vertical bricks were recessed in the patio walls, creating a pattern of rhythmically perforated surfaces. In the north and south façade, the remaining vertical bricks were also slightly rotated, further enhancing the filter effect. As if there were not enough brick patterns, the courtyards also received a floor covering made of herringbone-bonded bricks. The only other visible material is the wood of the beamed ceilings, floors and window frames. Not noticeable, however, are the steel plates and cables concealed in the load-bearing brick walls.

Thanks to the openwork masonry, a play of light and shadow, which changes with the position of the sun during the day, emerges inside. Thus, the studio is shielded from the outside world without being completely disconnected from it. In a quirky way, the ubiquitous brick appears warm as well as ascetic, taking on the function of a filter; with its different textures it has an almost woven quality. Graciela Iturbide lovingly calls the building her "small factory of bricks." [ab]

The three equally large spaces stacked on top of each other are flanked by two courtyards.

While the house seems monolithic from the outside, the open, perforated structure becomes apparent on the inside.

Jury statement

"A small and delicate place between party walls, which manages to travel from the access to the roof in a harmoniously suspended manner between the two courtyards located at the ends. The houses in the Barrio Niño Jesús in Mexico City usually have only one or two floors. In the three-story Iturbide Studio, the different spaces are manifested very intensely, connecting the street and the ground floor with the city skyline where the diverse and lively roofs of the buildings coexist with the treetops.

An exercise of professional maturity, where the wise use of the properties of the brick allow going from full to empty and from opacity to a magical and ethereal porosity, consequently achieving a permanent balance between the different atmospheres of the inhabited interior and exterior."

Large sliding doors open on all floors to both patios.

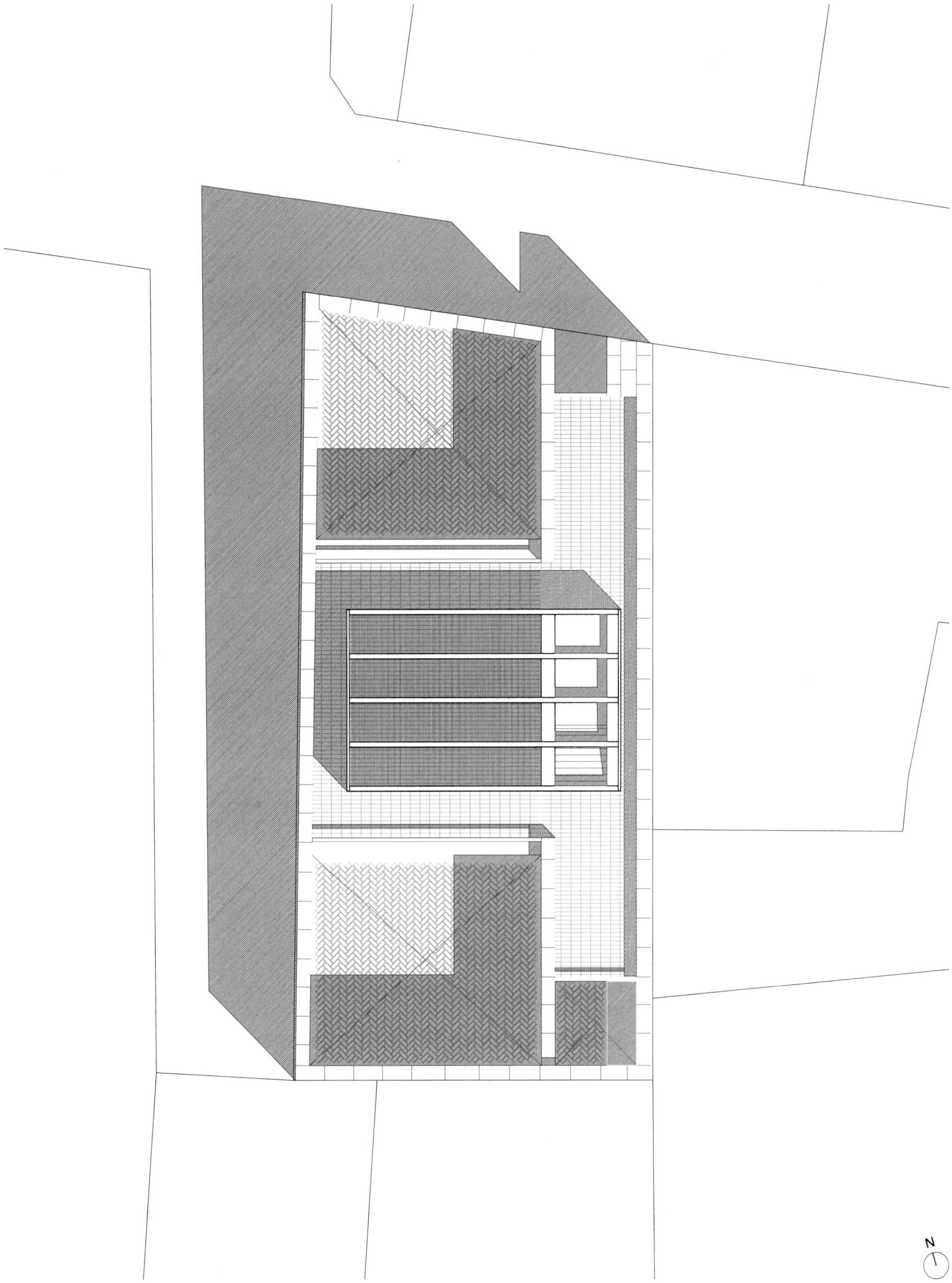

Roof plan

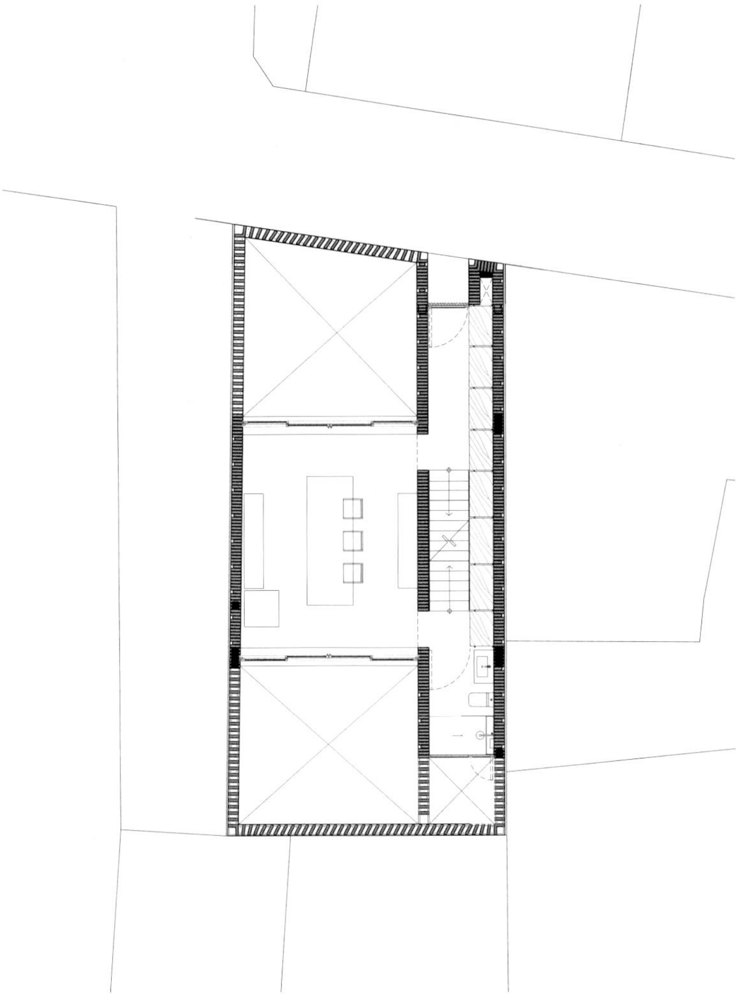

Second floor

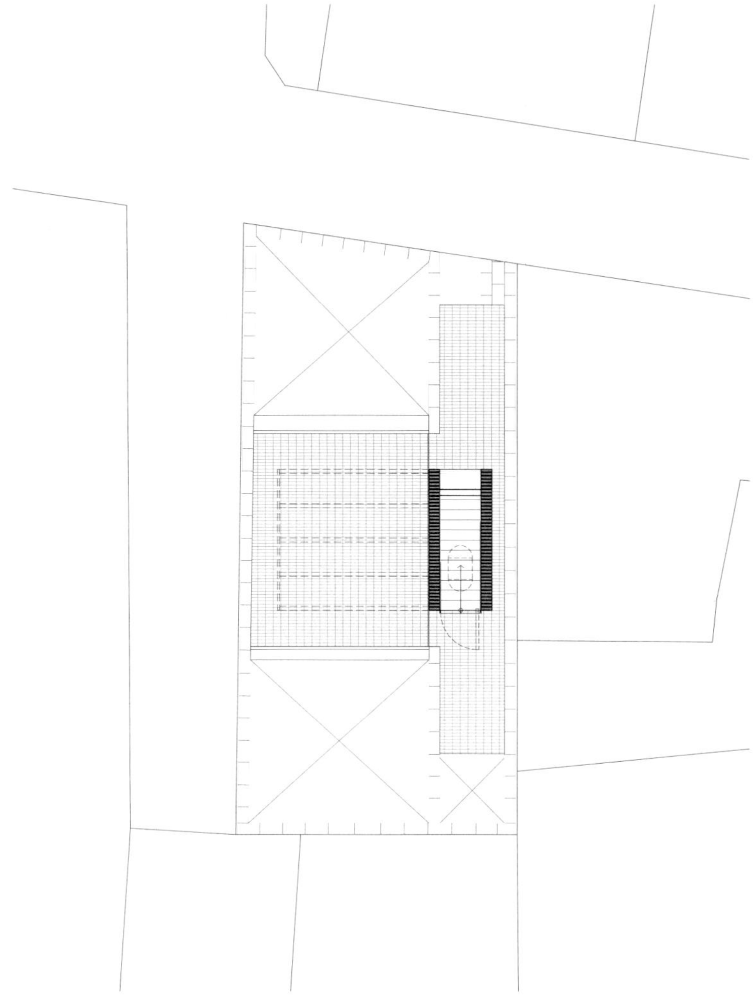

Third floor

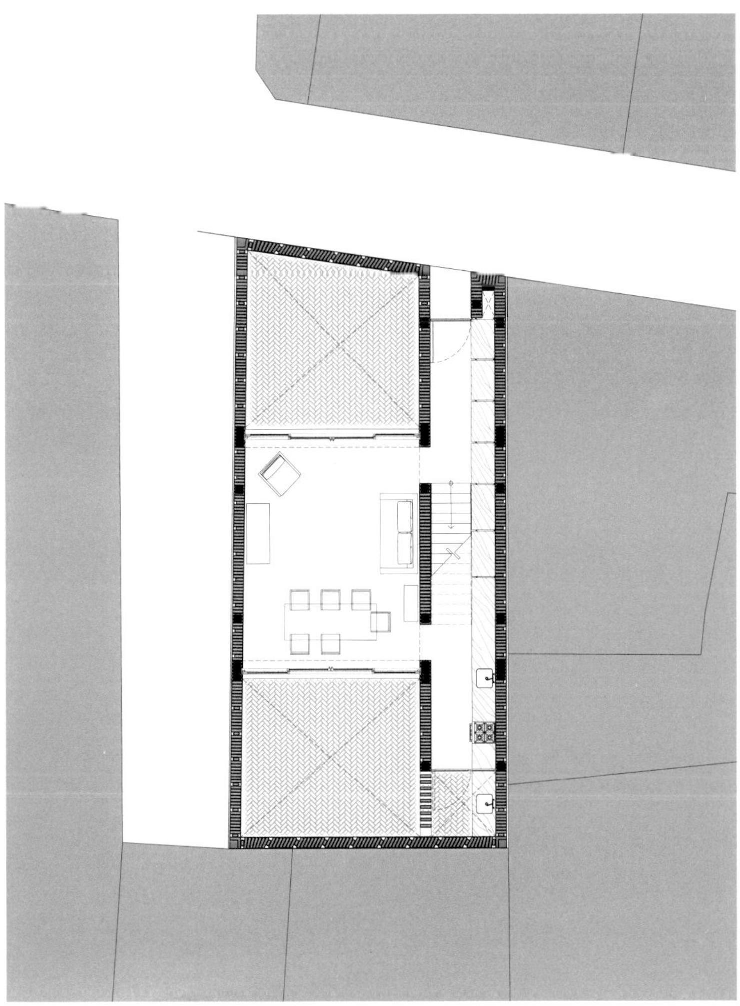

Ground floor

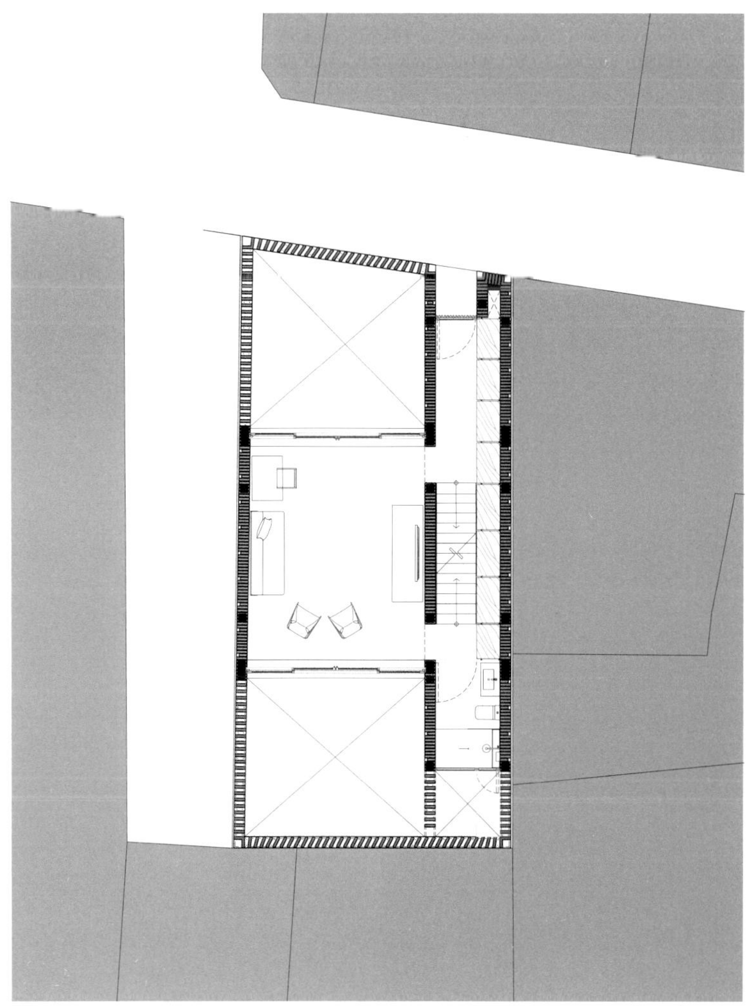

First floor

Can Jaime i n'Isabelle

Jaume Mayol and Irene Pérez

PROJECT NAME
Can Jaime i n'Isabelle

ARCHITECT/S
TEd'A arquitectes, Palma / Spain

BUILDING PURPOSE
Single-family housing

LOCATION
Palma, Spain

CONSTRUCTION PERIOD
2014–2018

BRICK TYPE
Clay blocks, facing bricks, paving bricks

BRICK AWARD CATEGORY
Feeling at home

BRICK 20 Special Prize Winner

Located on a gently sloping hillside, this single-family house in Mallorca interprets the classic type of courtyard house in a contemporary manner. The spatial concept of the monastic cloister was also taken up in this house. Understood as a patio and cloister, the courtyard fulfills a whole series of important functions: It is a point of intersection and a place of encounter, concentration, peace and quiet—a spiritual and material shelter. Moreover, it is ultimately an important element of building which is adapted to the climate.

In the models the TEd'A arquitectes refer to, architecture is built upon a square, without having to strictly and dogmatically follow geometry. Sealed off from the outside for the most part, the classic courtyard houses reveal a variety of spaces, paths, plants, closed, open and covered places: arcades, porches, terraces. TEd'A arquitectes also use this type to fit the house into the landscape: Stones of the property are integrated in the outer concrete walls; with the green roofs, the house becomes a part of the cultural landscape that is carried forward with it. It is partially dug into the southwesterly slope, so it does not obstruct the view of the landscape from the road heading northward.

Connected to the central courtyard, the brick-paved focal point of the house, are four further courtyards, laid out as gardens, which bedrooms, living spaces and kitchens are assigned to. A circumferential corridor connects all of the zones. Running once on the courtyard side, once along the outer wall, it offers a view to the south and an unsurpassable vista of the plain.

The spaces follow the course of the slope, resulting in a variety of visual references and volumes that make the house appear exceptionally lively.

> "Tradition passes on secular knowledge from generation to generation. Let's try to make the most of it and take it to a higher level."

The construction design and the building materials are applied with great directness and coordinated so that the interior spaces look like outdoor spaces pulled inwards—and the other way around. The house should not be perfect, but be able to incorporate the traces of use. Therefore, the supporting structure of concrete beams and ceilings is visible; the walls are made of bricks, partly out of clay bricks. They are painted white in the interiors; in the exterior spaces their bright, reddish earth tone is slightly softened with slurry, so that the craftsmanship communicated by the bricked walls does not disappear, but also does not come to the fore in a dominant way. Clarity and diversity, the eye for the beautiful detail and for the house as a whole have been combined here with great empathy. [ch]

Courtyard house and cloister: Both typologies are connected here.

The robust roughness of the surfaces helps the house fit perfectly into its surroundings.

Jury statement

"A house in an isolated location where the relationship between the different spaces is determined by the Mediterranean climate and the subsequent traditional architectural articulation and control with an intelligent use of the four courtyards.

The clay of the bricks is manifested in these spaces in its natural state and color, so that they illuminate the white-painted interior walls like a lantern, opening definitively from the main pieces to the outside.

Bricks in the vertical plane and terracotta in the horizontal, which, in contact with the skin, activate and place value on other materials: concrete as a structural complement, wood for door and window frames, but, above all, the outer sky cut by the different voids.

The use of brick is especially valued for the fact of building a place that, using its own resources and reinforced by the passage of time, will develop a pleasant microclimate, a habitable oasis, at different times of the year."

Colors and materials are used in a reduced manner in the interior.

Site plan with floor plan

Model

HEHNPOHL ARCHITEKTUR BDA

House at Buddenturm

Christian Pohl and Marc Hehn

PROJECT NAME
House at Buddenturm

ARCHITECT/S
hehnpohl architektur bda, Münster/Germany

BUILDING PURPOSE
Single-family housing

LOCATION
Münster, Germany

CONSTRUCTION PERIOD
2016–2018

BRICK TYPE
Facing bricks, roof tiles, paving bricks

BRICK AWARD CATEGORY
Feeling at home

Bold incisions made into the dark red and brown clinker brick façade of this gabled town house offer views along a narrow and characterful city street to the Buddenturm, a mid-12th century tower and the oldest surviving fragment of Münster's fortifications demolished for the most part at the end of the 18th century.

"Historical context, modern form, man-made materiality"

Used variously as a gunpowder store, a water tower and a control box for electric street lighting, the Buddenturm has chartered the history of this venerable quarter of Münster. The House at Buddenturm is, in turn, a knowing and subtle play on the city's architectural history: It is, at once, old and new, a modern concrete framed house that, with its crafted brickwork and steep gable, pays quiet homage to centuries of expressive if well-mannered historic buildings that make the kind of German city street it occupies such a pleasure to walk along and, in this case, to live in.

Here, references to history are elemental rather than literal. Arranged over four floors, the house proves to be surprisingly bright inside. Judiciously positioned skylights, slits, chutes and windows bring daylight and a play of shadows into and through generously planned rooms with their exposed brick and concrete walls and warm timber floors. The same windows make further connections to Münster's history, one of them framing a perfect architectural view of the Protestant University church, a design of the late 17th century built for the Franciscans and rebuilt in the 1950s after extensive war damage.

The house makes the most of what had been a vacant site. There is a garage behind bronze doors at street level, while living spaces project out over the pavement and open right up into the gabled roof space. Interiors are, in fact, both generous and adventurous with hints, perhaps, of German Expressionist design and even of inventive concrete and brick German churches of the 1950s and 60s. At the same time, these are evidently serene spaces and made special not least because, inside and out, the House at Buddenturm has a strong and comfortable sense of materiality: it is solid and reassuring as well as thoughtful and quietly original, qualities enhanced by the use of dark facing bricks on the exterior along with paving bricks and clay roof tiles. With this brickwork, the house is visibly all of a piece and very much a part of the enveloping townscape.

What Marc Hehn, Christian Pohl and their Münster-based team have done so well here it is to show how a very traditional form of city house can be reinvented for the 21st century without recourse to painting-by-number historicism. [jg]

Lively plays of light are created by elements placed on the wall in a slanted manner.

Section

The shape and color of the bricks are also found in the neighborhood.

The brick facing of the window reveals mark the transition to the outside.

ATELIER VENS VANBELLE BVBA

Stephanie & Kevin

Maarten Vanbelle and Dries Vens

PROJECT NAME
Stephanie & Kevin

ARCHITECT/S
atelier vens vanbelle bvba, Ghent/Belgium

BUILDING PURPOSE
Single-family housing

LOCATION
Haaltert, Belgium

CONSTRUCTION PERIOD
2016–2017

BRICK TYPE
Clay blocks, ceramic façade panels

BRICK AWARD CATEGORY
Feeling at home

A terrace house at the end of a cul-de-sac, at the transition to the landscape—a beautiful task for architects. Often, the potential of such a location is not lived up to and the standard solution is chosen, which, in the case of this house, cannot be asserted by any stretch of the imagination. On the contrary: What the architects Dries Vens and Maarten Vanbelle from Ghent have planned and realized here in Haaltert, a small town between Brussels and Ghent, is not only shaped by the special location, where the coverage transitions into the landscape. No, the light and playful architecture is literally bursting with life. Incidentally, the house carries the first names of the owner-couple.

It is organized as a split level parallel to the street, with the structure of the offset story ensuring that the house for the family of four did not have to be built with a basement. Nonetheless, a semi-underground area for ancillary rooms became possible.

The bright area for family life can be reached from the entrance hall via the mezzanine staircase. Integrated into the floor offset, but not reaching up to the ceiling, the built-in furniture divides the space into zones without separating the kitchen from the living area. Because the upper floor in the rear has also been set slightly upwards, the kitchen, glazed along the entire width of the house towards the garden, becomes higher. Light from the roof terrace falls into the part of the living room situated in the depth of the building, making it sufficiently bright there, too.

The three-dimensional thinking that underlies this house also manifests itself in the wooden parquet, which leads from the floor across the walls, and also covers the underside of the ceiling. The open area is thus separated from the upstairs bathroom and bedroom—as white cubes, they appear as if they were placed into the space.

"Bricks can be light, bright and playful!"

Functionally, the house is clearly divided in a horizontal fashion: into a storage area and laundry, an open family space and a more intimate realm for withdrawing. This can likewise be read on the outside: The plinth is made of concrete blocks; the living area is glazed on three sides thanks to slim steel columns; the upper floor is clad with bright and yellow-glazed facing clinkers. This unusual combination of materials prevents the closed upper floor from weighing heavily on the main floor.

The house gains a light, pavilion-like quality, which corresponds terrifically with the landscape. The arrangement of the facing clinkers in a grid form provides clarity and precision, carefully balanced with the collage-like effect of the various materials and the lively split-level organization. The roof and terrace parapets are covered in glass so that the sky is reflected in them—not only was the transition to the landscape at the end of the street considered, but also the one to the sky. [ch]

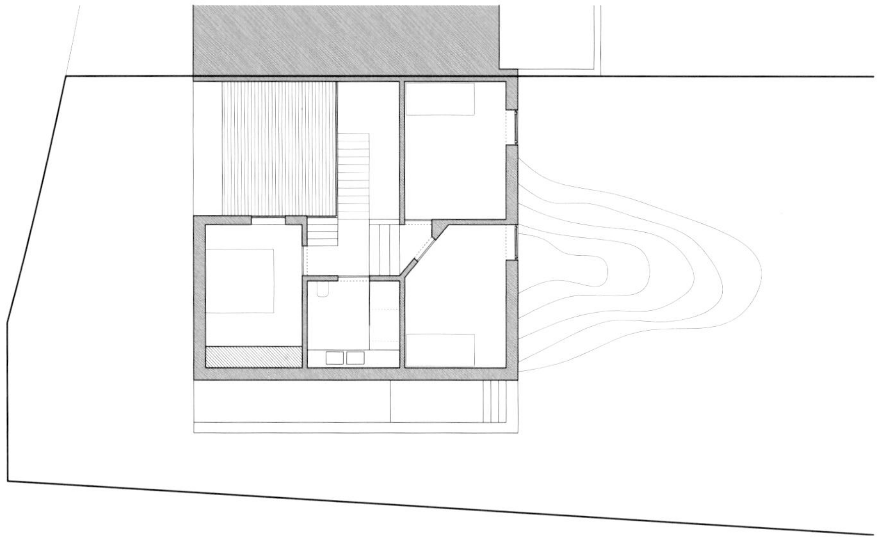

Level +2

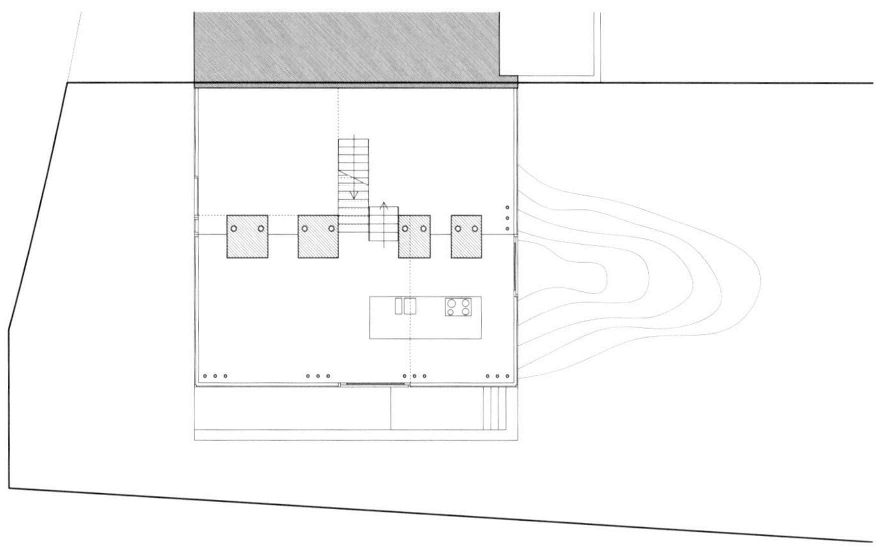

Level +0.5 and 1

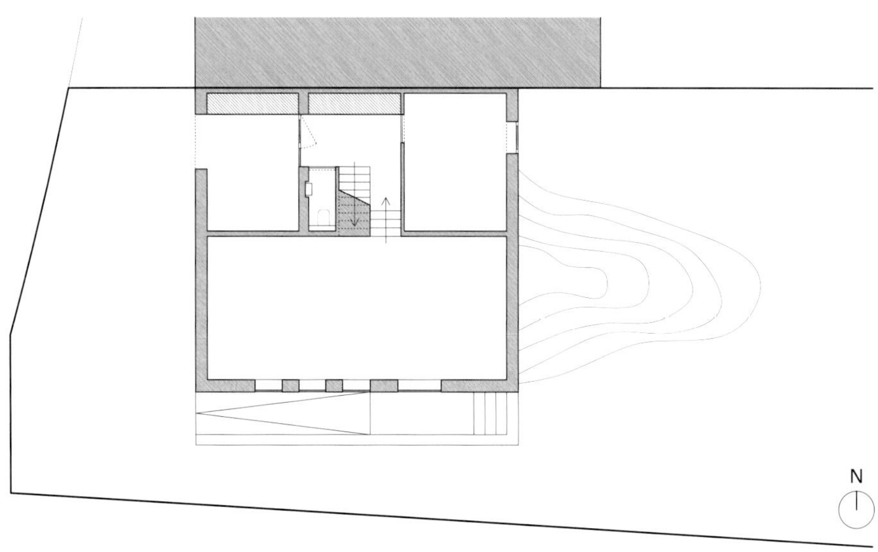

Level -0.5 and 0

Ceramic façade panels like the ones on this house are increasingly being used in architecture again.

The kitchen is located on the middle level.

H&P ARCHITECTS

AgriNesture

Doan Thanh Ha

PROJECT NAME	LOCATION
AgriNesture	QuangNinh Province, Vietnam
ARCHITECT/S	CONSTRUCTION PERIOD
H&P Architects, Hanoi/Vietnam	2017–2018
BUILDING PURPOSE	BRICK TYPE
Single-family housing	Clay blocks
	BRICK AWARD CATEGORY
	Feeling at home

AgriNesture is a hollowed out seven-meter cube framed in concrete and clad in brick. It is also a radical new type of house in the context of Vietnamese cities where space is at a premium and nature too often excluded. A double-skinned wall of locally made clay brick forms the structure of the house. The space, or buffer zone, between the two skins helps to keep AgriNesture cool in summer, warm in winter and pleasant during Vietnam's humid spring.

For H&P Architects, AgriNesture is a prototype that the studio hopes will be reproduced in clusters with trees growing between individual homes.

> "A house which helps to promote agriculture and at the same time creates jobs for local residents."

The interior of each AgriNesture house can be different from its neighbor. It could offer just one cavernous room or several rooms across its two floors. All houses, however, would be provided with roof gardens to grow vegetables and, if desired, steel lattices fixed to the exterior walls for climbing plants. Collectively, clusters of such houses would create communities both urban and rural. As a concept, AgriNesture is a riposte to rapid and formless urban sprawl. The nest metaphor, say the architects, evokes something between dwelling space and cultivated land.

The essence of the AgriNesture house is simplicity, affordability and versatility. Touchingly, the prototype has been built for a former coal miner, a bachelor who now revels in the high and light space of his home, an environment wholly opposite to the one he knew day-to-day working underground. With a need for just one bedroom, space had been given over to growing plants inside the house and to a vegetable garden on top.

Since the studio was founded in 2002, H&P's mission has been that of "Architects for the Poor." Poverty is measured not simply by low incomes, but by the loss of rural areas to urban residential development. This goes ahead with little or, more usually, no respect for nature and no sense of how people can grow their own food in urban areas. Equally, because much new suburban development is realized on a mechanized or semi-mechanized basis, it involves precious little use of locally produced and recycled materials. AgriNesture is a way of building low-cost homes in tune with nature and suited to the earning power and way of life of most Vietnamese people and especially to those millions of people who have been forced, through economic factors, from the countryside to the city with no wish to abandon rural knowledge and skills. All requirements that are fulfilled by bricks. [jg]

AgriNesture in a cluster

The double-shelled brick structure provides for a good indoor climate and vegetables can be grown on the roof.

The high void makes the small house spacious and bright.

JFGS / JOSÉ FRANCISCO GARCÍA-SÁNCHEZ

Casa Jacaranda

José Francisco García-Sánchez

PROJECT NAME
Casa Jacaranda

ARCHITECT/S
JFGS / José Francisco García-Sánchez, Almería / Spain

BUILDING PURPOSE
Single-family housing

LOCATION
Almería, Spain

CONSTRUCTION PERIOD
2017–2018

BRICK TYPE
Facing bricks, clay blocks

BRICK AWARD CATEGORY
Feeling at home

The pristine white brick and concrete walls of Casa Jacaranda rise from an earth and stone terrace overlooking Las Negras, an old fishing village, and the Gulf of Almería, a stretch of the Spanish Mediterranean coast protected from insensitive modern development. The sculptural cliffs and craggy hills of the Cabo de Gata-Níhar Natural Park embrace the gulf. Despite the uninterrupted horizon of an azure sea, this is a desert landscape, the driest place in Europe. It is home to wild olives, wild boar, rosemary, thyme, snakes, flamingos, salt works and jacaranda.

"Jacaranda House explores the possibilities of handmade brickwork built irregularly."

Casa Jacaranda has a clear-cut simplicity and yet its walls are clearly formed of handmade bricks and roughcast concrete painted white and yet textured. Although rigorously planned, this is a Mediterranean house and clearly at home in this gloriously demanding landscape. It is not some industrial machine for living in.

During the construction of the house, José Francisco García-Sánchez has been at pains to create surfaces that reveal the imprint of the human hand. Here, the knowing "imperfections" of the brickwork encourage plays of small shadows while providing toeholds for darting or sunbathing lizards. This effect is enhanced by the way in which the bricks are arranged in courses of different spacing and depth.

Built on a sloping site, the entrance and garage are above a ground level incorporating a pool. On the uppermost floor, a lattice of brick and concrete pillars protects bedrooms from the glare of the southern sun. The structure of the house is also designed to deflect strong winds like the Siroccos that sweep across the bay from the Sahara in spring and autumn.

Casa Jacaranda shows how new houses can be placed in natural settings while responding both to climate and to an age-old tradition of building white houses with flat roofs and white walls along the Mediterranean coast. Looking at this example, it seems somehow significant that Le Corbusier—to whom, along with Mies van der Rohe, it owes a debt—studied Mediterranean architecture so his own designs became more naturally or roughly textured.

Overlooking the Gulf of Almería, José Francisco García-Sánchez has found a balance between the natural, traditional and modern worlds of both landscape and architecture. It is no surprise to discover that the architect was born in Níjar, a "white" village less than 15 kilometers from Casa Jacaranda, nor that his studio is in Almería. "If you want to be universal," he says quoting Leo Tolstoy, "shout from your village." [jg]

A luxurious reinterpretation of a Mediterranean house

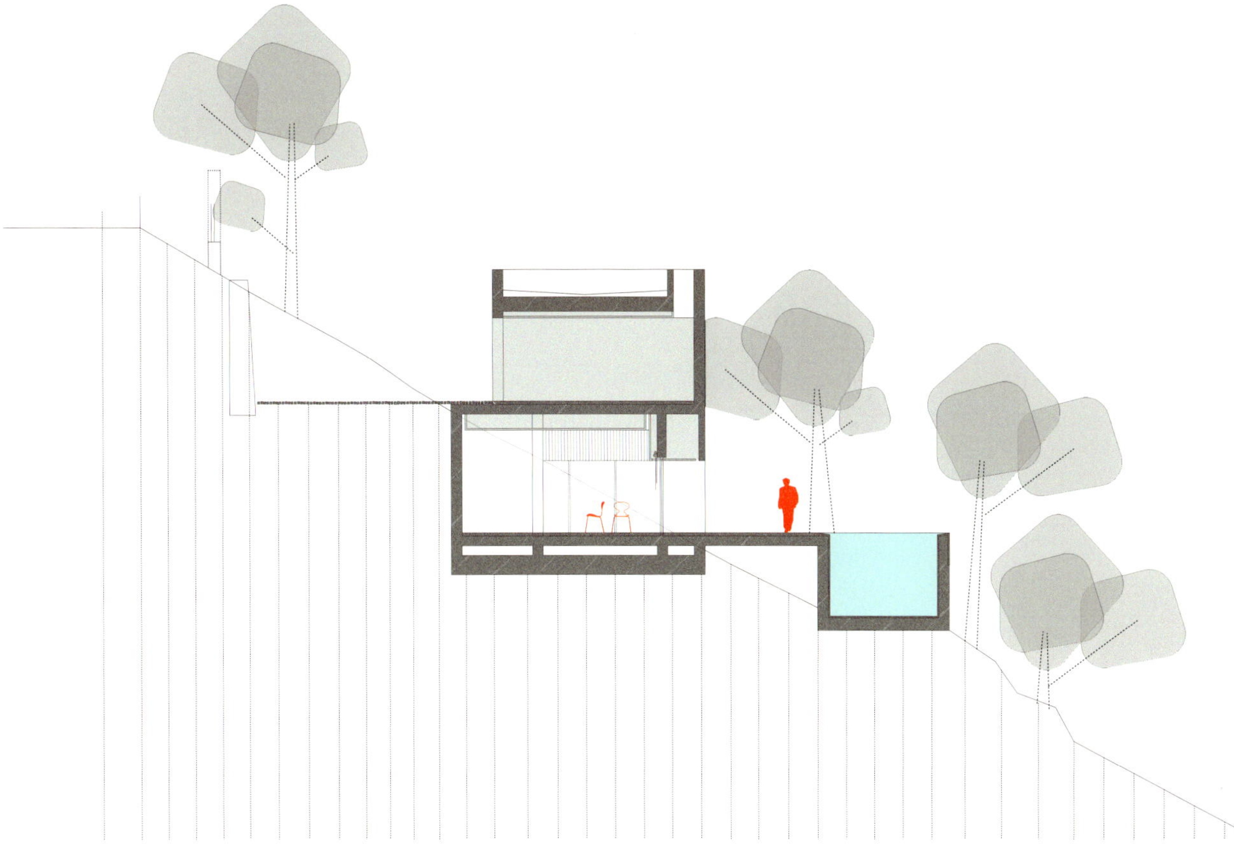

Cross section

DOSA STUDIO

Palmas House

Sergio Sousa and Raúl Medina

PROJECT NAME
Palmas House

ARCHITECT/S
DOSA STUDIO,
Mexico City/Mexico

BUILDING PURPOSE
Single-family housing

LOCATION
Texcoco, Mexico

CONSTRUCTION PERIOD
2017–2018

BRICK TYPE
Clay blocks

BRICK AWARD CATEGORY
Feeling at home

Building a simple house that is more than just a dwelling remains one of the most important tasks for architects to this day. Sometimes, given the abundance of impressions and possibilities, it may be a question of how much or how little of a house a person really needs. In the vast majority of cases, however, it is about a building that can provide a dignified home with few resources, even for those for whom it is not a matter of course, because they are simply poor. In this sense, the architects see the Palmas House as a social project: it shows how a good building can arise with simple possibilities.

> "Architecture can improve life conditions that must not depend on large budgets."

It was built in Texcoco, Mexico for a family that had lived for several decades in a—as usual in Mexico—self-built house. This was a rather makeshift dwelling, which had serious shortcomings in terms of exposure and ventilation, as well as with regard to construction. The family eventually sought the support of the architects, who accepted the mission and the challenge. It was a matter of finding a form for multigenerational living, in a simple way and on a tight budget, which not only offers well-lit and well-ventilated spaces, but also takes equal account of the need for intimacy and community. Founded in 2014 by Raúl Medina and Sergio Sousa, the Dosa Studio office actually succeeded in planning a new and decent home for this family with partially donated building materials.

Completed in 2018, the house is located near the center of the city of Texcoco, northeast of Mexico City. It is flanked on one side by a garage, on the other by a courtyard through which the house £can also be entered. The simple, single-leafed and reinforced masonry construction of red and reddish-black bricks determines the appearance. The reddish-brown painted steel frames of windows, shutters, exterior doors, staircases and ultimately the water tank placed on the roof create a uniformity that stands out from the usual bricolage aesthetics of the surroundings and the dominating gray of the other house walls. The floors and the roof are made of bricks inserted between concrete beams.

However, the material is not an aesthetic end in itself: Thanks to its storage capacity, it acts like a temperature buffer on the cold nights and hot days that characterize the climate here. White-glazed bricks were only laid in the kitchen and the bathrooms for the sake of better usability. The built-in furniture is made of simple laminated veneer lumber; the roof is composed of three consecutively arranged sheds, whereby each of the three bedrooms still has a skylight in addition to the opening to the courtyard. [ch]

The unplastered or unclad visible surfaces determine the character of the house.

Built-in furniture made of laminated veneer wood completes the range of used materials.

A simple and nonethelss well thought-out house that also has asthetic qualities

226ARQUITECTOS

Casa Joven

Tristán Bondone, Luciano Femopase and Julian Genesio

PROJECT NAME
Casa Joven

ARCHITECT/S
226arquitectos, Cordoba/Argentina

BUILDING PURPOSE
Single-family housing

LOCATION
Cordoba, Argentina

CONSTRUCTION PERIOD
2016–2018

BRICK TYPE
Facing bricks

BRICK AWARD CATEGORY
Feeling at home

The outskirts of San Francisco in the eastern part of the province of Córdoba, hot and humid in summer, are not exactly picturesque. Founded in 1886 as an agricultural colony and home to Italian refugees, the town itself grew from the 1940s with the arrival of piped water. Pasta factories, dairy farms and metal workshops made their mark. San Francisco continues to grow with a demand for low-cost homes especially for young people.

The Casa Joven is an attempt to create a new type of low-cost house in an uncertain setting of empty building lots and construction sites on the edge of San Francisco. Built with 30,000 bricks, this house — its walls reinforced with concrete columns and beams to resist earthquakes and powerful winds — has a box-like, double height space serving as a living room, kitchen, dining room, workroom and bedroom. It feels far more generous than conventional low-cost homes with their narrow street frontages, deep plans and claustrophobic arrangement of compact rooms.

Alongside this principal room is a bathroom, then a garage with a mezzanine bedroom above it. This is meant for children. Across the entire front of the house is a perforated, double-height, brick screen designed for privacy, as well as to defuse noise and to reduce the intensity of sunlight from the west. A gap between the screen and the house itself is what the architects call a "galería," a room of sorts open to the elements that helps create a distance or breathing space between the house and its matter-of-fact surroundings.

"Despite being a millennial material, brick can still offer new alternatives and solutions as it was done in this house."

From these simple devices, Tristán Bondone, Julian Genesio and Luciano Femopase of 226 arquitectos have shaped a house of intelligently modest sophistication alive with dappled daylight and ever-changing shadows. Throughout Argentina, brick itself is a traditional, low-cost and readily sourced local material, and yet the architects have demonstrated how, deftly arranged and laid, these can raise a modest house from a matter-of-fact building to a work of elemental architecture.

The architects aim to live up to their name in projects however modest: 2.26 is the measure Le Corbusier gave to his "modular" system of proportions derived from the height of a man with his hand raised and employed famously in the design of his Unité d'Habitation housing scheme in Marseille.

With houses like Casa Joven, the sprawl of towns like San Francisco could yet feel purposeful and even attractive, and certainly so to young people with high standards but little money hoping to set up home. [jg]

The brick lattice in front ot the façade provides privacy as well as sun and noise protection at the same time.

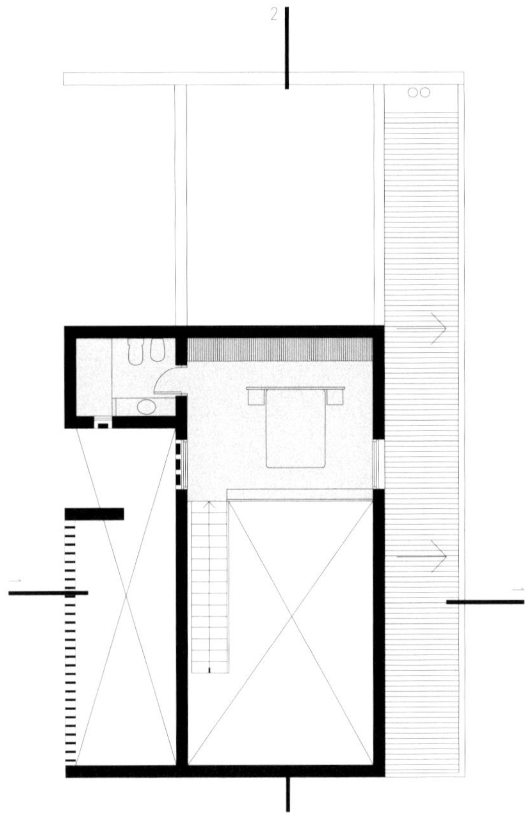

Upper floor

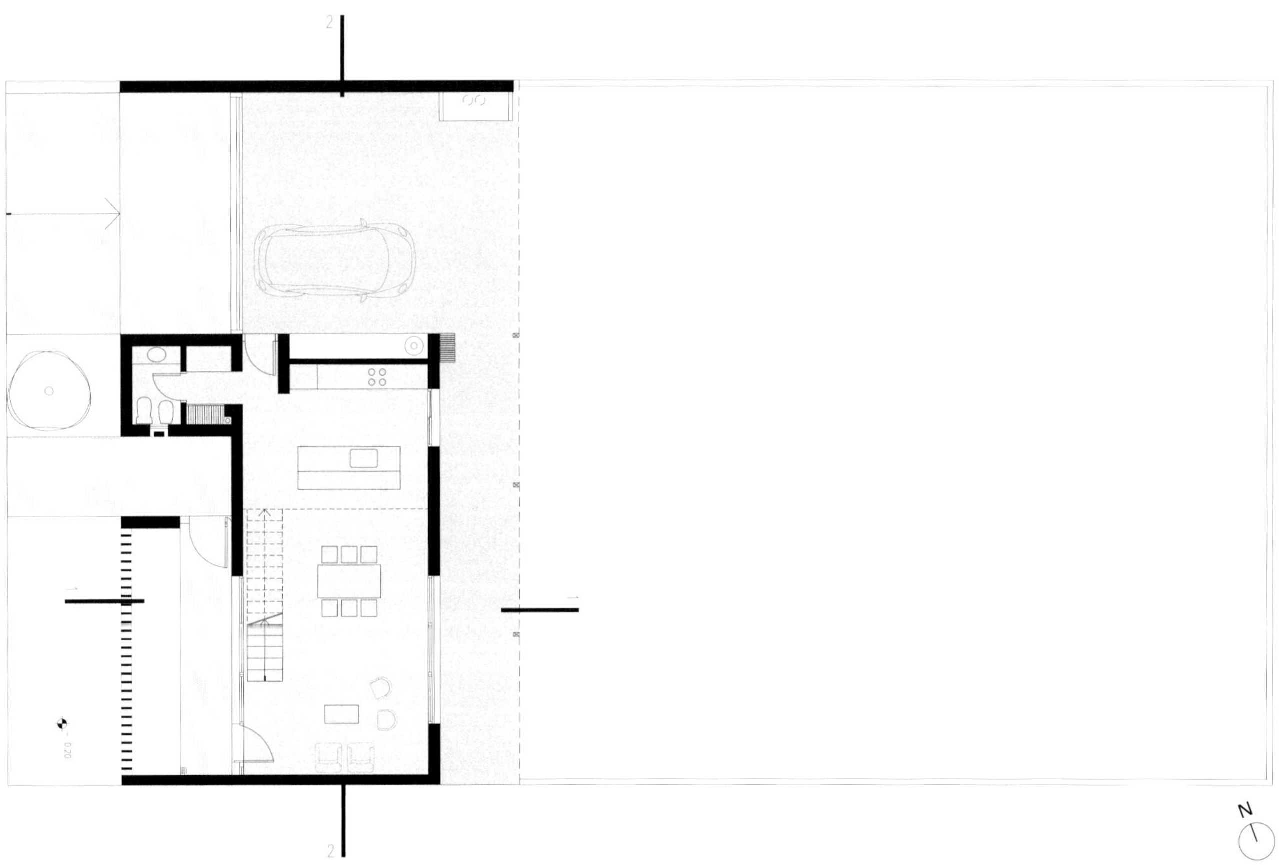

Ground floor

The interstice is an almost intimate arrival zone.

ESTUDIO BORRACHIA

Casa en Canning

Alejandro Borrachia

PROJECT NAME
Casa en Canning

ARCHITECT/S
Estudio Borrachia, Buenos Aires/ Argentina

BUILDING PURPOSE
Single-family housing

LOCATION
Canning, Argentina

CONSTRUCTION PERIOD
2017

BRICK TYPE
Facing bricks, paving bricks

BRICK AWARD CATEGORY
Feeling at home

The white house stands as an autonomous object on the green meadow in Canning, a suburb of Buenos Aires. Almost completely without visual cover, it offers neighbors and passers-by a seemingly unimpeded view into its inner life. It is regarded as a built landscape in which architecture and the environs merge.

> "We think of this house as a replicable typological system or model of inhabitation on the city outskirts."

Based on a grid of 3.5×3.5 meters, the house has a square-shaped building area measuring 14×14 meters in total. The entire house is organized around a patio located in the middle. All of the rooms surround the central courtyard and form a clockwise sequence from openly visible spaces to private, closed ones.

Situated on the south corner, the entrance is marked by an open-brick screen behind which a planting bed and a bench can be found. The structure is raised about 30 centimeters on piles above the meadow, emphasizing its object-like quality. One first enters the covered terrace, which then leads to the outdoor kitchen with a barbecue and dining area. This is followed by the living room with a kitchenette, which in turn heads to a corridor that provides access to two children's or guest rooms, and the master bedroom. The tour ends there.

Both the terrace and dining room are covered and opened not only to the outside, but also to the inner courtyard, maintaining the character of a gallery rather than a room with their narrow steel columns and a light roof. Only the private areas—living room, bedroom and bathroom—have closed walls made of white-painted brick.

The house in Canning is to serve as a prototype for suburban living, which could be mass-produced in the future. Therefore, the architects opted for a brick-filled metal construction that is inexpensive and quickly reproducible. All horizontal surfaces, such as floors and ceilings, are clad in wood. Rosé-colored, thick-sized brick was also used for paving the driveway and covering the patio.

Brick was not only used as a technically suitable and artistically expressive material, but also as part of the energy and climate concept, since it serves as a storage mass and ensures a balanced air humidity, which contributes significantly to the well-being inside the house.

It's all about simplicity, modularity and gradations between openness and closeness—a bit like a further development of Le Corbusier's Dom-Ino House. Thanks to the detached structure and white color, the steel and brick radiate a pleasant lightness. [ab]

The lightweight atrium house is a prototype for suburban living.

Transparent, semi-transparent and closed elements alternate with one another.

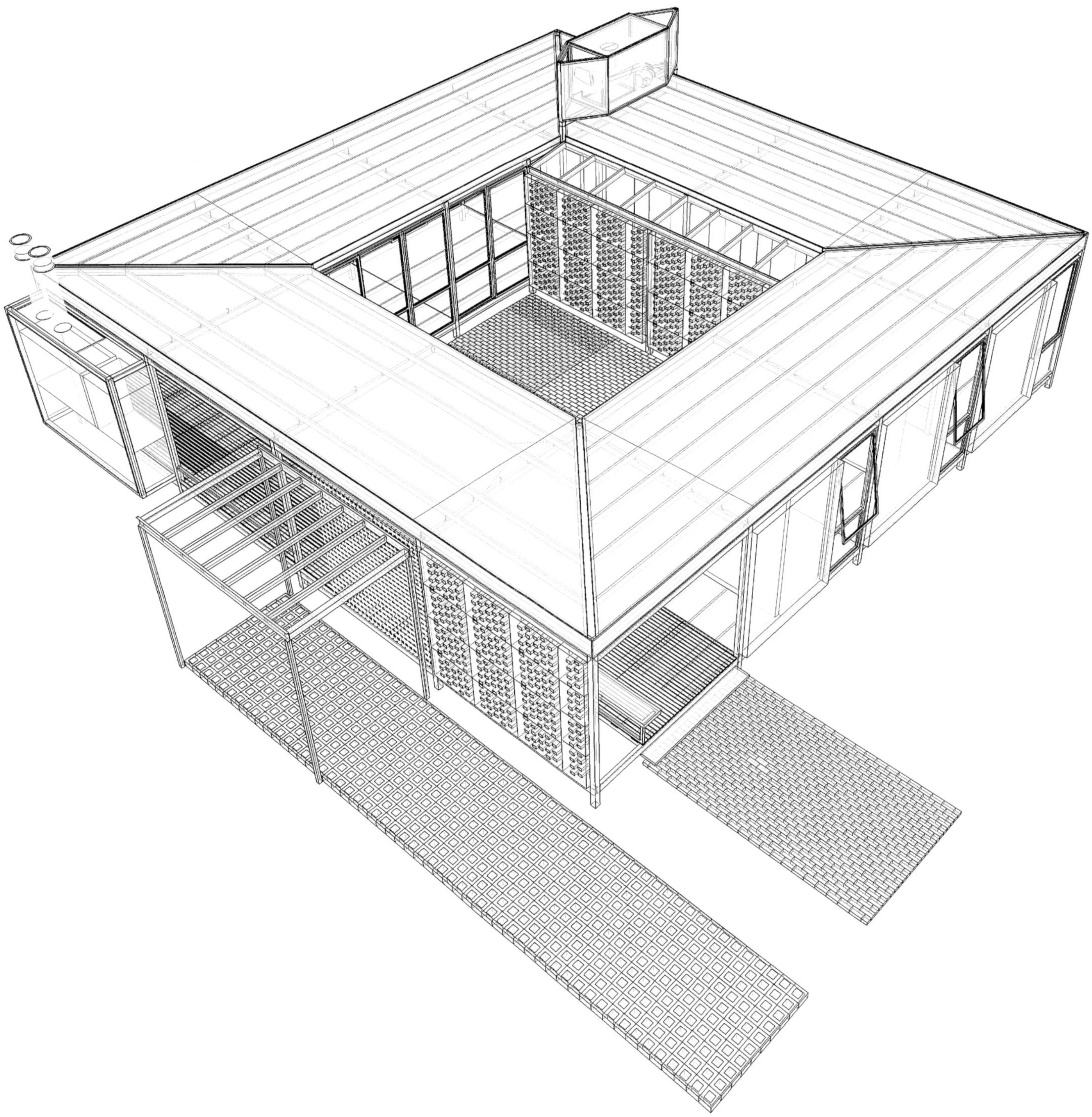

Axonometry

The brick is a part of the energy and climate concept.

The modular construction method guarantees low-cost reproducability.

H&P ARCHITECTS

Brick Cave

Doan Thanh Ha

PROJECT NAME
Brick Cave

ARCHITECT/S
H&P Architects,
Hanoi/Vietnam

BUILDING PURPOSE
Single-family housing

LOCATION
Hanoi, Vietnam

CONSTRUCTION PERIOD
2017

BRICK TYPE
Clay blocks

BRICK AWARD CATEGORY
Feeling at home

The Brick Cave is a two-story, double-skinned family house in Thuy Lâm, a northern suburb of Hanoi, a thousand-year old city growing rapidly today. Its architects, Doan Thanh Ha and Tran Ngoc Phuong, have made the perimeter of the building's site synonymous with the house itself. Not a square millimeter has been wasted in terms of providing maximum accommodation for its occupants. Far from lacking greenery, however, the Brick Cave features a rooftop vegetable garden, while between its perforated brick skins there are spaces for plants to grow. Unexpectedly, the house—a permeable membrane despite its apparent rock-like solidity—is open to nature.

Hanoi's climate is tropical, so the ideal house must breathe in the wet heat while fending off frequent rain. The Brick Cave is well-suited to these testing environmental conditions, although despite its name, it is a light and bright home behind its double brick skin. But while offering generous views out from the windows of its sloping walls, it provides occupants privacy. The garage is enclosed within the walls, so that once a car is driven inside and the entrance closed, the house is a private cocoon.

As for the brickwork, this has been produced by a local factory, meaning that precious little energy has been expended on the making of this low-energy use home. By night, the prismatic and filigree façades of the house make it glow like a lantern, a casket of light that helps make a suburban street the stuff of architectural sorcery rather than anonymous sprawl.

"Artificial nature structure"

The atrium-like ground floor is an uninterrupted and generous space for living, dining, playing and praying. Bedrooms and bathrooms are on the 2nd floor and the vegetable garden above them. The voids between the skins of the house are double height to allow trees to grow inside. As they expand, their branches can stretch out through the outer skin. Over the years, the building will become a frame for vegetation as much as it is a home.

The destruction of vast tracts of tropical rainforest during the prolonged Vietnam War and the subsequent loss of trees and greenery as Vietnamese cities have expanded has encouraged architects to think increasingly of ways in which cities can green themselves. Recently, the Vietnamese solution has been to grow trees around and inside new buildings. The Brick Cave is one adventurous way of doing this. [jg]

The roof garden is an answer to the missing green space in Vietnamese cities.

Trees growing between the double-shelled brick wall

Brick Cave occupies the whole plot area.

GRAUX & BAEYENS ARCHITECTEN

House L-C

Koen Baeyens and Basile Graux

PROJECT NAME
House L-C

ARCHITECT/S
GRAUX & BAEYENS architecten, Ghent/Belgium

BUILDING PURPOSE
Single-family housing

LOCATION
Anzegem, Belgium

CONSTRUCTION PERIOD
2015–2017

BRICK TYPE
Facing bricks, reused bricks

BRICK AWARD CATEGORY
Feeling at home

Outside of their cores, Belgian villages often dissipate into long roads with peripheral development, which sometimes directly transition into the next village. In the town of Anzegem, the House L-C also stands in such a row. Nevertheless, it has an exceptional position, since it marks the spot where the usual built-up area joins a group of detached, larger Belle Époque mansions emerging from the street line. It was therefore necessary to plan a building that could mediate between the two typologies on the empty, trapezoidal site.

A house with 240 square meters of living space, which is narrow and closed towards the street, but unfolds and opens towards the back of the property, thus arose. While the east wall connects to the neighboring house, the west wall is to form a distinctive end of the row, maintaining some distance to the old brick wall that indicates the border to the neighboring lot. It was formulated as the second main façade, in which the development strip zigzags around the corner. This generated a spatially interesting outdoor area, where a simple driveway would have otherwise laid.

The house encompasses three volumes with a square base, as well as the interstice that they form to the adjacent terraced house. Rotated by 45 degrees, the middle of the three squares touches the other two at one corner. Different ceiling heights enable the cubes to be even more clearly recognizable as separate units from the outside. Inside, on the ground floor, an office space is oriented towards the street; the dining room is located behind it, while the living room and the kitchen are situated on the garden side. On the upper floor, the bedroom, two children's rooms and the bathroom find place in two cubes. The transitions between the square spaces are openly designed and accentuated by the exposed concrete beams of the roof structure, resulting in an unusual sequence of spaces. A kitchenette, the staircase and a small, glazed niche with a view to the outside are tucked into the three remaining, acute-angled spaces.

"The house with façades of recycled bricks mediates between two typologies."

All lounges feature floor-to-ceiling windows. The upper floor street and side façades are largely closed, but the masonry opens up in vertical stripes at three strategic points, letting light fall into the spaces behind: the walk-in wardrobe, the staircase and one of the children's rooms.

The façades of the house are made of colorful, recycled, vertically-bonded bricks. Their colors change between light pink and brown, seemingly combining every brick variant of the neighboring buildings. With its modern design vocabulary and lively material, it forms an almost playful completion to the row of houses. [ab]

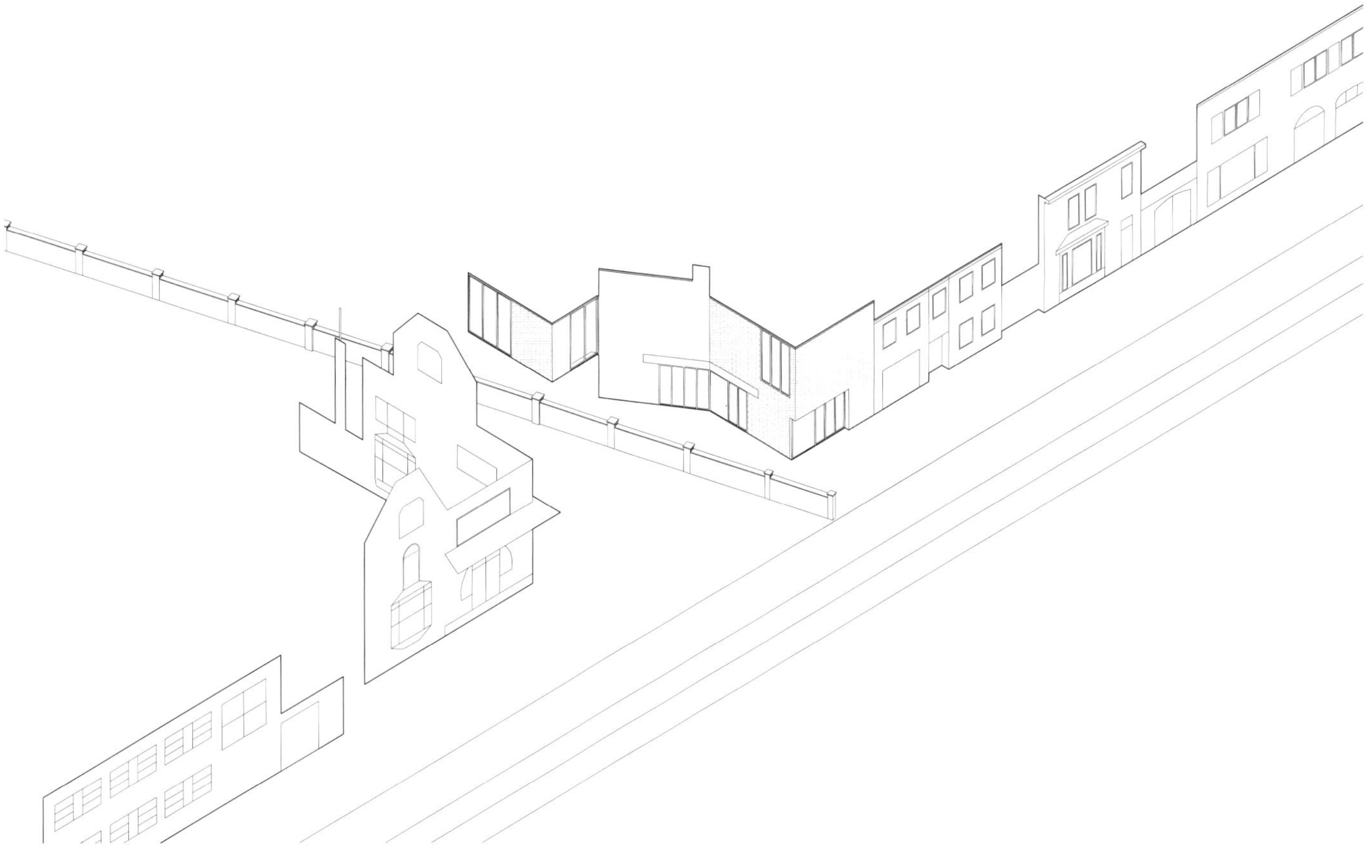

Street façade elevation

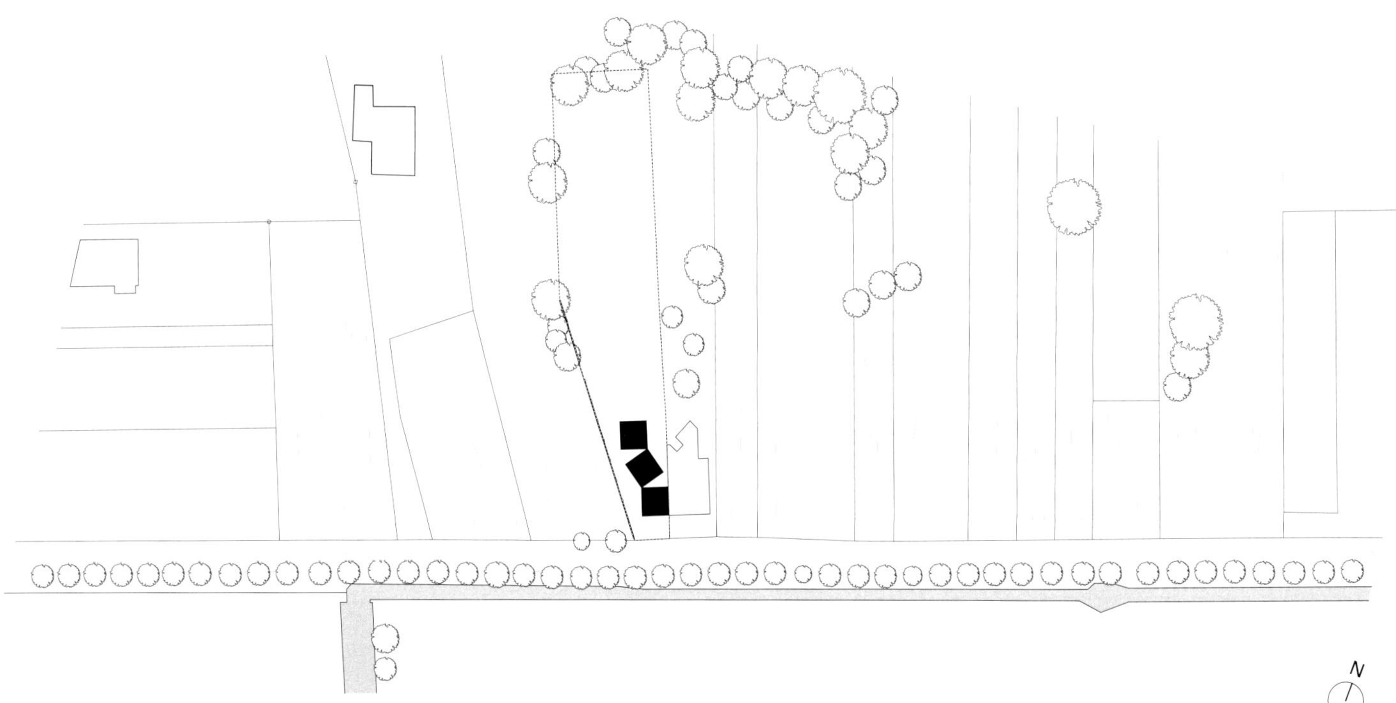

Site plan

The arrangement of the three cubes provides a spatial diversity not only in the building's interior.

The unusual structure of the house is a result of the transition between two development typologies.

Living together

JANA REVEDIN

Quiet and Green: The New City

Jana Revedin

Social structures and their various utilization demands, as well as urban planning and architecture with their architectonic struc tures, materials and technologies, are in rapid transition. The sustainable city, the sustainable rural area, must therefore be rethought in order to serve future generations as well.

Urban Ecology

In pre-industrial human epochs, habitats grew organically and were hence user-friendly and flexible. The cities of antiquity functioned as a socio-political learning process and made the *polis* and the freedom of the individual that prevailed here a model for the success of human history. Moreover, it was understood that cities should never become denser and larger than their natural environment allowed. A city was ecologically autonomous; it fed itself and recycled its waste cyclically and without an external energy supply. In the industrial age, this circular ecology was ruptured and the allegedly "progressive" production sites, growing rapidly on account of the rural exodus, were designed without properly taking people's needs into consideration. Time, our most valuable resource, was (erroneously) interpreted as money that ruled haste, according to Fordist principles.

It was not until the early modern age that the Bauhaus movement's reform architects made themselves into the rediscoverers of sustainable urban development: Walter Gropius, Bruno Taut or Ernst May, but also Adolf Loos, already postulated a climate-friendly construction according to "air, light and sun," an extendable "growing house" with "gardens for self-sufficiency" for an "actively lived green"—yes, indeed, a thoroughly modern "urban ecology." These reform planners thought holistically and interdisciplinarily again, listened to societal needs and favored the re-densification of existing urban spaces and the mixture of functions, instead of the "mechanical" separation of living, working and leisure. Max Weber called for a "social mixing of the cities" as a guarantor for living quality and cultural acceptance, for circular economies and circular ecologies.

Zoning: A Mistake of the Century

The clever, interdisciplinary criteria of the reform planners—the urban space was not designed *in silo,* but together with geographers, botanists, sociologists, writers, artists…—were lost as of the Charter of Athens of 1933. The Swiss architect Le Corbusier was able to assert his ideologies at the CIAM IV Congress, which took place in the year of Hitler's seizure of power and the immediate removal of all relevant architectural thinkers from official positions. *Tabula rasa,* straight from the drawing board; Le Corbusier separated living, working and all other activities into predetermined "zones." This "zoned" city, which also had to be "car-friendly" (instead of human-friendly) and locked its inhabitants in satellite towns full of "unités d'habitation," became the model of completely misinterpreted modernism. Starting from France, Le Corbusier's doctrine celebrated a questionable triumphant march through the colonial countries of the so-called Third World back then.

Sustainable Living Space

Traffic calming, actively used green space, subsidized rents, integrated transportation and communication systems, conscious settlements—all these are the tools available to us today to make up for this dogmatic mistake of the century. But political will is in great demand, because the world population has increased eightfold since then. The lively cultural re-mixing of society as we experience it today requires architects and spatial planners to constantly adapt according to the principle of "trial and error." There is no other way of reacting to the megatrends of climate change, migration, rural depopulation and a society in Europe that is overaging and tends towards impoverishment. Sustainable living space emerges in small steps, according to organic growth patterns, and in interdisciplinary cooperation.

Is the New City Quiet and Green?

When it comes to the sustainability factor of traffic calming, digital analyses of traffic and user flows help us beyond mere assumptions or "views" influenced by everyday or party politics. A prominent example of a scientifically sound working method is Jan Gehl's redesign of Times Square in New York, a noise-and traffic-plagued inner city plaza, which the city administration long did not want to liberate from the automobile, which was considered to be "vitally important." Here, digital analyses of traffic flows could prove that traffic calming is possible, that we can give people back their city squares in a "quiet and green" fashion. As a digital tool for social housing, on the other hand, "Hubitation"—software solutions for startups of smart home or smart meter applications—is recommended.

Learning from the Global South

The once-maligned Third World has developed into a pioneer in sustainable thinking, as a more permeable norm and rule canon allows for more innovation. Emerging design "rebels" are inventing refreshing solutions, such as the Pritzker Prize winner Alejandro Aravena, who, out of the prevailing lack of budget, is simply building social living quarters in Chile that are only half-finished. The residents themselves complete construction according to their own needs, whereby the supporting basic structure and the vital infrastructure of the buildings, including the transportation and digital connections, are provided by the housing associations. People are no longer pushed to the city outskirts and their cultural and social roots are respected. Every user becomes—based on Hannah Arendt's model of *homo faber,* the busy, creative person—an active co-creator.

"Radicand" Designing

Such participatory approaches are also finding more and more imitators in Europe: non-profit housing associations increasingly recycle existing—and thus inherently sustainable—properties, with architects, political and economic decision-makers and future residents pondering in advance about which new programs are really *necessary.* In our design theory, we use the term "radicand" for this. Urban space and living space may again grow organically, rooted in many ways, and in rhizomes, just like the radicand plants, ivy, strawberries... The method is based on the practices of reform modernism and involves first the common "co-programming," then the "co-design," and finally the "co-execution." We give users time to define their needs, a lot more time than is afforded by "top-down" program catalogues. Usage changes must be taken into consideration from the beginning, because architecture, as Walter Gropius said, is "service to society." Our works are not eternal and inviolable, but rather live and change with the people.

REFACCIONES AUTOMOTRICES
GONHER

RAFI SEGAL, MIT RWANDA WORKSHOP TEAM

Prototype Village House (The Umusambi House)

Rafi Segal

PROJECT NAME
Prototype Village House (The Umusambi House)

ARCHITECT/S
Rafi Segal, MIT Rwanda Workshop Team / USA

BUILDING PURPOSE
Prototype single-family housing

LOCATION
Kigali, Rwanda

CONSTRUCTION PERIOD
2017–2018

BRICK TYPE
Facing bricks, clay blocks

BRICK AWARD CATEGORY
Living together

BRICK 20 Category Winner

Rwanda is the most densely populated country on the African continent, but at the same time very rural, with only 26 % of its inhabitants living in cities. Outside the urban areas, a sprawl of small houses covers the hilly landscape.

Because such peri-urban settlements also require modernization and expansion, a state program to promote village development has existed since 2013. These projects, however, are centrally managed, do not involve the local population and resources, and result in uniform new buildings with high construction costs. To develop an alternative, a team of MIT Africa students headed by Professor Rafi Segal conducted a three-week project in the village of Mageragere, west of Kigali. Together with villagers and local laborers, they worked out a prototype for an affordable house, the modern, efficient architecture of which is completely tailored to Rwandan needs.

Commensurate to the standard of the village construction program, the house stands on a 100-square-meter plot. Its elongated shape is ideal for the hilly terrain, as relatively little ground needs to be excavated to build the house. On the inside, the structure offers about 68 square meters of freely separable living space, as Rwandan families are often large and sometimes several families share a house. Since much of the housework and family life traditionally takes place outside, a total of 86 square meters of land has been covered. A combination of closed and open masonry emphasizes this transition between inside and outside, as well as provides natural lighting and ventilation. A rainwater harvesting system collects the water draining from the pent roof and eliminates long hikes to public water points.

"A step towards modernization from within traditional building"

The wall system of the house features a core of panels made of compressed straw fiber combined with 10 × 10-centimeter-thick concrete posts. Unlike most Rwandan village houses, it was not clad in sun-dried bricks, but with longer-lasting red ones. These were supplied by the Swiss company SKAT Consulting, which operates kilns near the village and also organized tours there for local construction workers and residents during the construction period.

Initially, only a single structure with a pent roof was built as part of the pilot project. In the future, the houses are to respectively stand back to back in pairs, so that they can share a chimney, a water reservoir and a wall, which in turn reduces construction time and material costs. The goal is to even build entire villages of the new house type, which thereby takes on an urban scale. This small brick house could, therefore, have a big impact. [ab]

A prototype will be built for the time being; the houses are to be constructed in pairs in the future.

Model of a double unit

Village structure

Jury statement

"The Prototype Village House from Rwanda is a new housing typology explored. The buildings can be combined in pairs and laid out in a variety of ways to form different urban patterns.

The small house has a loadbearing steel structure but uses locally made brick for the walls and benches. Its design is a result of both economical and aesthetic decisions and every detail is thought through to create an affordable, beautiful and sustainable living space. The layout of the plan is simple yet refined. The roof is tilted to create more space in the entrance patio and living room. The sloping roof also harvests rain water and collects it in a reservoir in the lowest part, where it ends in a tall brick structure that creates natural ventilation for the kitchen and bathroom area.

The waving roof lines and the punctuating chimneys give the rows of houses a nice rhythm that resonates with the surrounding village and the trees."

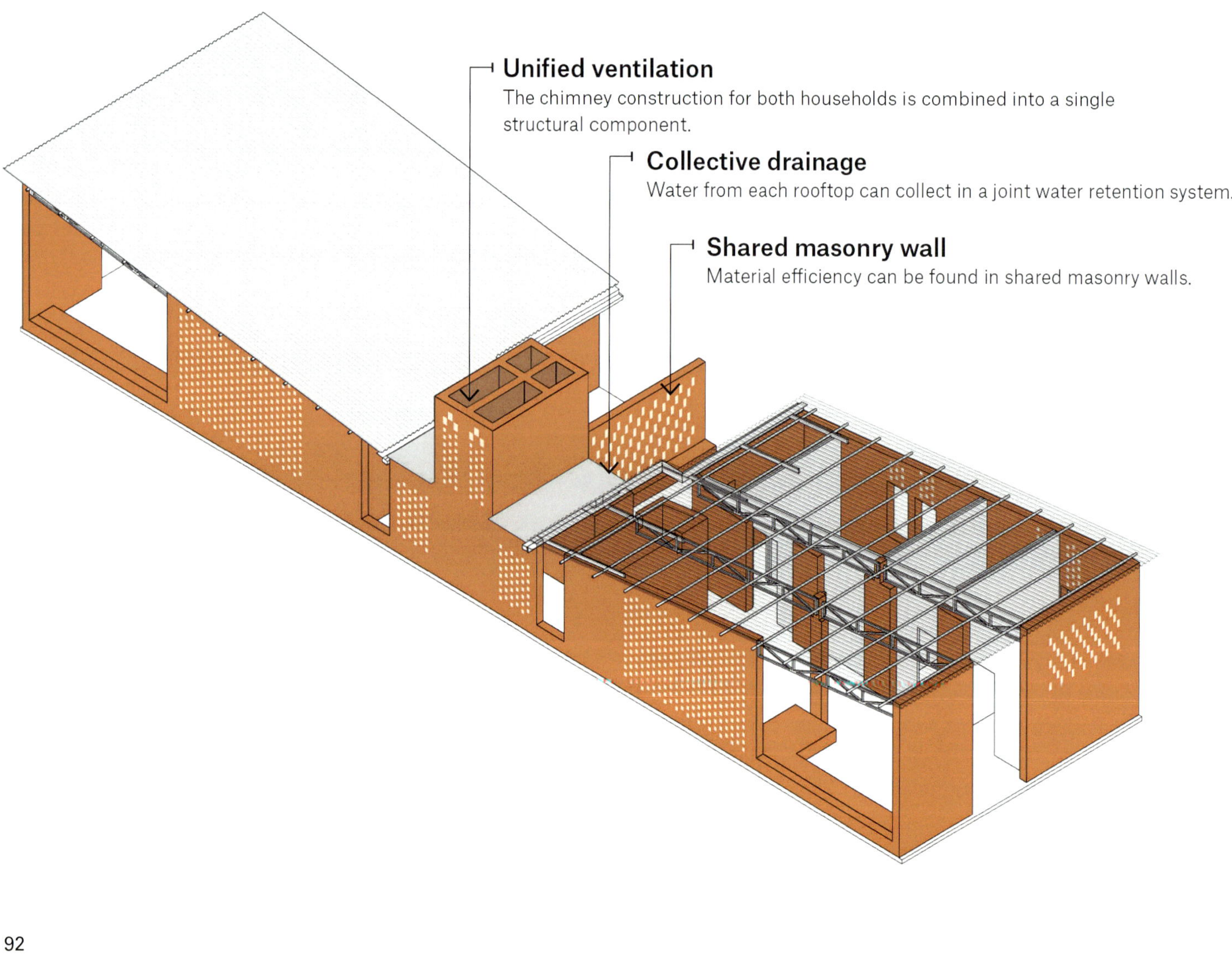

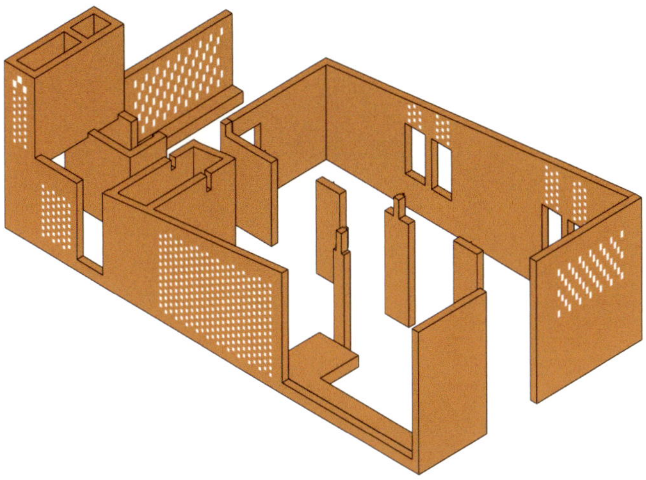

Brick structure

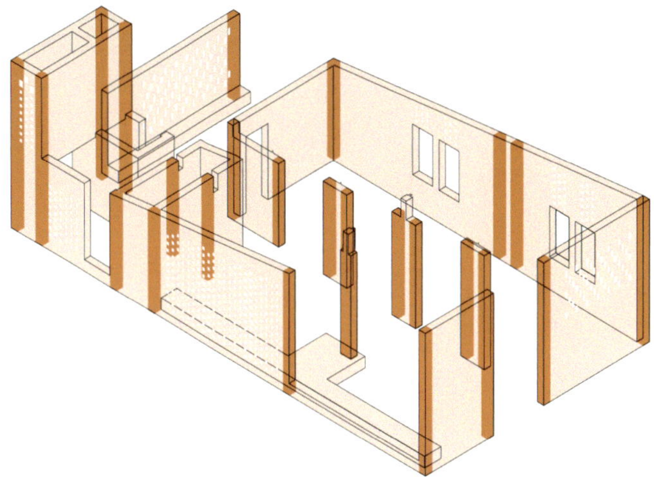

Embedded support structure

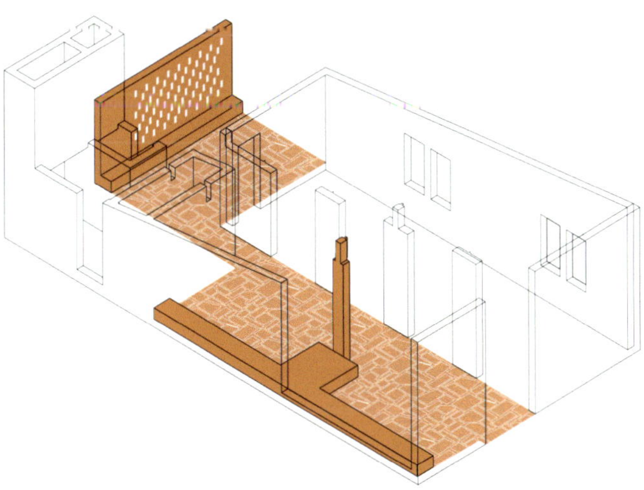

A covered porch at the front and an exterior court at the back of the house

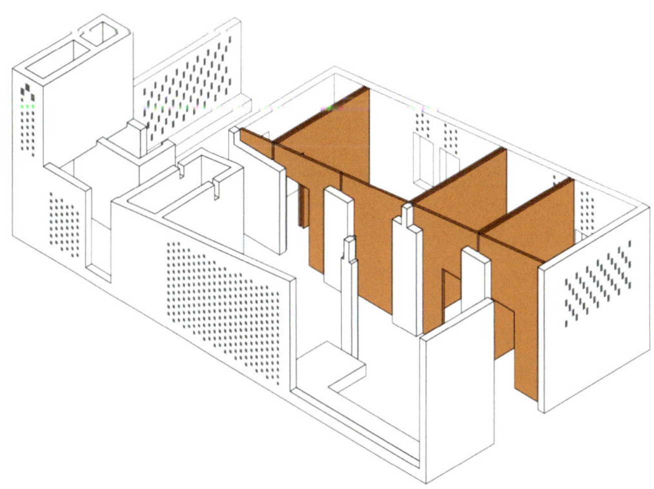

Self-arranged interior partitions allow for flexibility in the number and size of rooms.

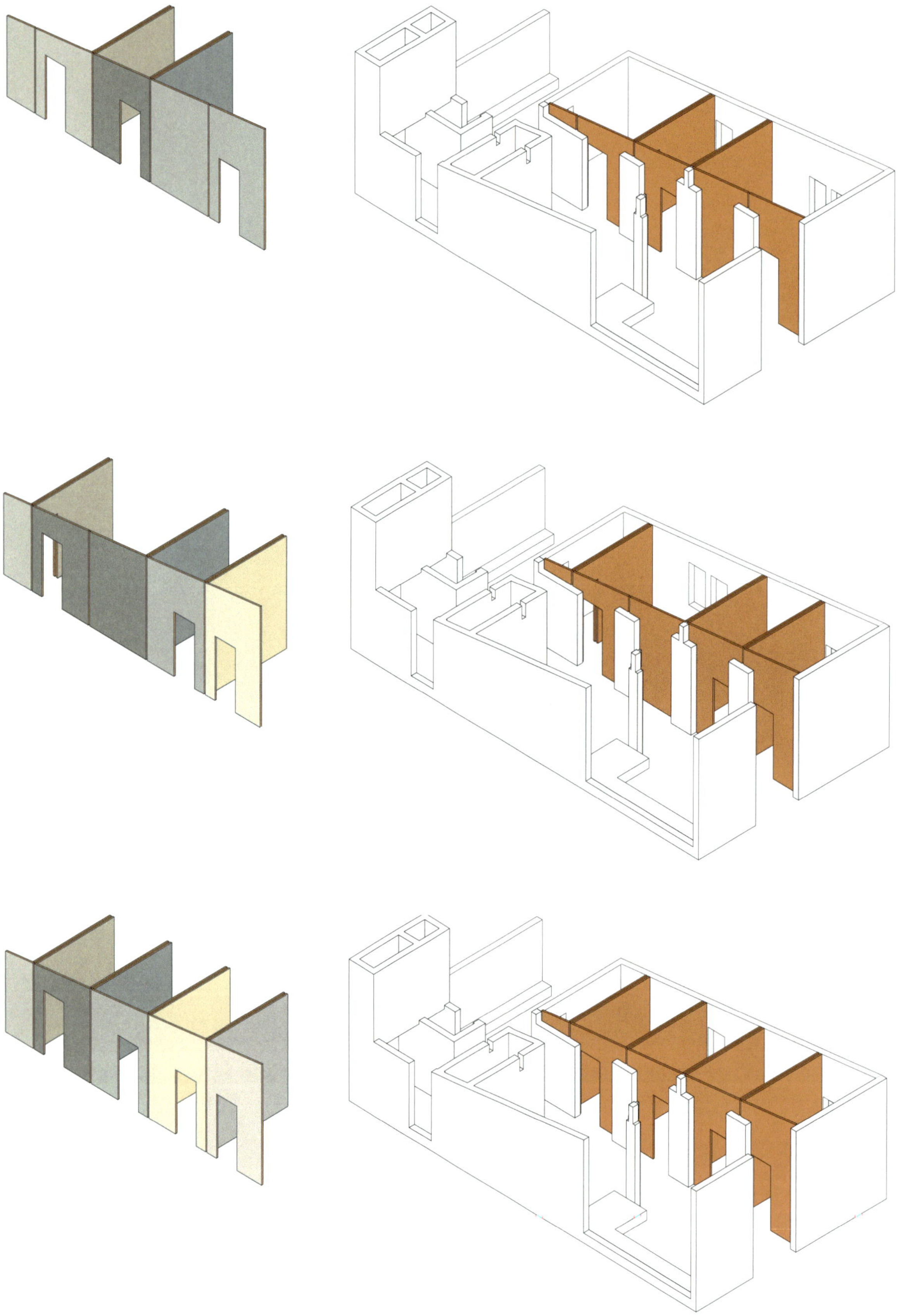

Different variations of room arrangement

FUNDAMENTAL APPROACH ARCHITECTS

Saadat abad Residential Building

Mohsen Kazemianfard

PROJECT NAME
Saadat abad Residential Building

ARCHITECT/S
Fundamental Approach Architects, Tehran/Iran

BUILDING PURPOSE
Apartment housing

LOCATION
Tehran, Iran

CONSTRUCTION PERIOD
2016–2018

BRICK TYPE
Facing bricks

BRICK AWARD CATEGORY
Living together

BRICK 20 Honorary Mention

Clear ideas for the conversion of a seven-story house with two basement floors were laid out by the client: It should be a residential building for open living, yet take the needs for protected privacy into consideration. For the architects this meant that both would be achieved primarily by the façade: an unobstructed view to the outside and an interior shielded from insights. What did not make the matter easier was the context. The street side is the only one the house can be opened up towards. Because the block on which the house stands is narrow, there is only a tight gap on the rear side to the house on the other side of the block. The staircase is also placed here—too narrow for a pleasant view.

> "The space between the twisted brick skin and the glass is called the expanded border."

The Fundamental Approach Architects team invented a façade that brings the interior and the exterior into a special relationship. Instead of a hard border in the form of a conventional solution with small windows, they found one that creates a transitional area, an extended threshold between inside and outside. Returned to its supporting structure, the house received a completely new skin for this purpose.

Towards the street the implemented apartments feature floor-to-ceiling glazing. Protruding slightly, the floor slabs leave a narrow strip for plants. A further layer of prefabricated panels with a perforated brick structure reminiscent of paravents was added in front of them. They are partly mounted parallel to the glass façade, partly rotated out of this plane. In some cases fields remain free, giving the impression that the façade has been cut open and bent, or that its elements have been twisted outwards here and there. The direction of the panels is chosen so that the view is guided towards the nearby intersection. At the same time the incidence of light is varied by the different directions of the panels, since the openings in them appear smaller from the inside the more inclined the panels are arranged. Depending on the position of the sun, a single element enables a diverse light mood inside. Since the floor-to-ceiling glazing lets itself be opened, the living space can also become a loggia.

In two layers, the slender bricks are attached to a metal structure in a way that makes them barely perceptible. As the bricks of the panels are moreover arranged in staggered planes, a surface strongly structured by light and shadow, looking as if knitted, is generated when the sun shines. No longer perforated, this brick structure continues on the interior walls and on the entrance area of the house. To solve a task well, sometimes you do not need many ideas. They only have to be good. [ch]

Honorary mention:
"The jury found the project uses brick in a poetic manner, so that the façade appears to be somewhat fragile, seemingly pried open, an equally simple and innovative solution."

The stucture of the brick panels is also reflected on the inner wall.

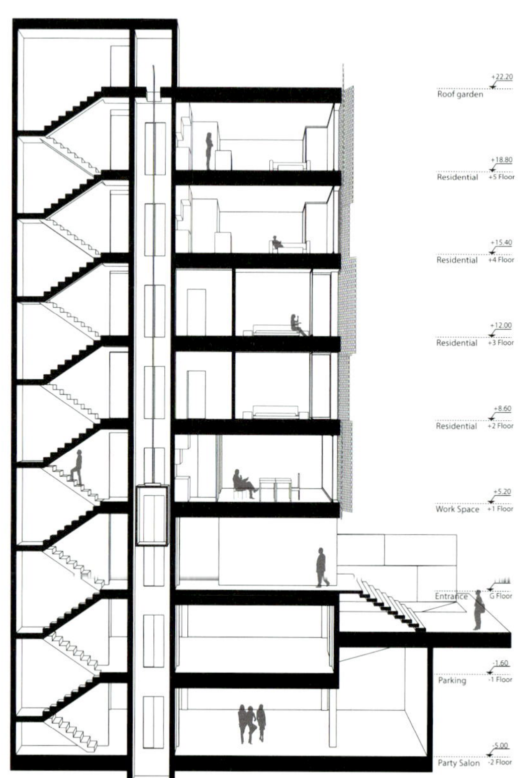

Section

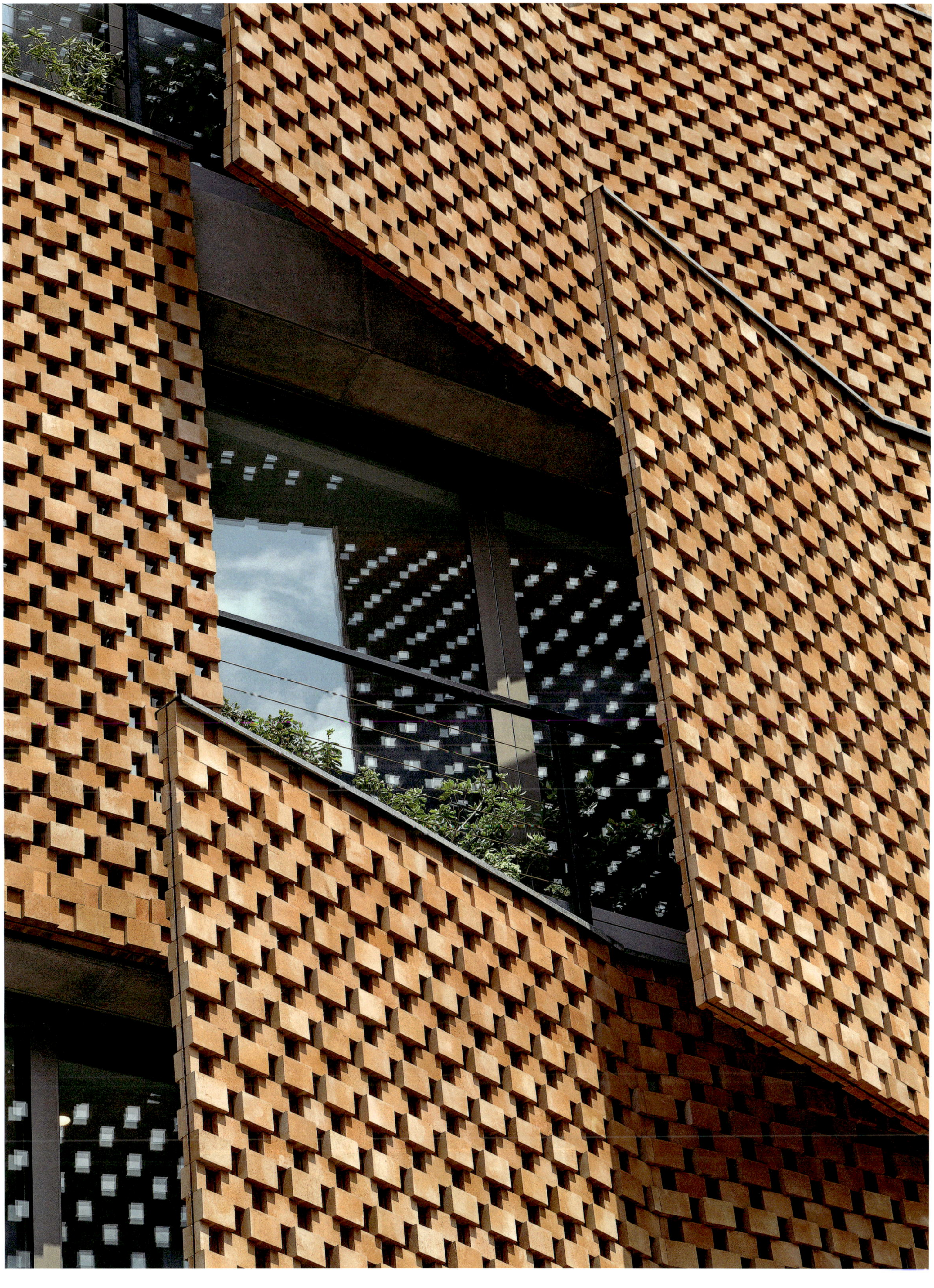

ATELIER KEMPE THILL

High-Density Low-Rise Spijkerkwartier Arnhem

André Kempe and Oliver Thill

PROJECT NAME
High-Density Low-Rise Spijkerkwartier Arnhem

ARCHITECT/S
Atelier Kempe Thill, Rotterdam / The Netherlands

BUILDING PURPOSE
Apartment housing

LOCATION
Arnhem, The Netherlands

CONSTRUCTION PERIOD
2016–2018

BRICK TYPE
Facing bricks, paving bricks

BRICK AWARD CATEGORY
Living together

Located northeast of the city center of Arnhem, the Spijkerkwartier is a residential neighborhood built in the late 19th century. An ensemble of 16 minimalist, white terraced houses stands out between the historic homes, almost like a village enclave in the city. Atelier Kempe Thill designed them as a typological experiment: affordable houses with gardens were to be integrated into the urban context, combining low height with urban density. Beyond that, it was about testing the relationship between privacy and collectivity, as well as between individuality and homogeneity.

"The new brick type solves the architectonic problem of the expansion joints."

The building volume consists of four parallel strips, each with four terraced houses that look almost identical on the outside and are separated by walled gardens. Two clusters of bicycle garages or garden sheds are arranged between the rows of houses. The house and shed façades are made of a yellowish-white brick with a centered flute, which gives the ensemble a distinct identity. Thanks to the flute, the freestyle bond appears as a tile bond that cleverly integrates the expansion joints so that no difference between the non-loadbearing house façades and the loadbearing garden walls is recognizable. This enhances the external homogeneity of the quarter, which is also separated from the outside area by a walled green strip.

On the inside, the houses, which each feature about 150 square meters of living space, offer a surprising amount of flexibility. While the north façades are designed in a rather closed manner, a 4.50 x 3.10-meter-large void lies behind the south façades, which are completely glazed, equipped with large sliding doors, and face the garden. A free-standing staircase leads from there to the first floor. A maximum of five bedrooms could be distributed within this base structure. Moreover, the future residents were able to choose between a number of different door, stair and bathroom types during the planning process.

For the window frames, the architects used brown anodized aluminum, combined on the south side with solar control glazing and integrated gray blinds. These are the only materials that deviate from the whitish brick. With this consequent leitmotif, the architects successfully kept residents from setting up their own fences and sheds from the DIY store. A minimalist complex that marks a harmonious balance between unity and diversity was thus created — at a construction price of only 900 Euros per square meter. [ab]

Site plan

Upper floor

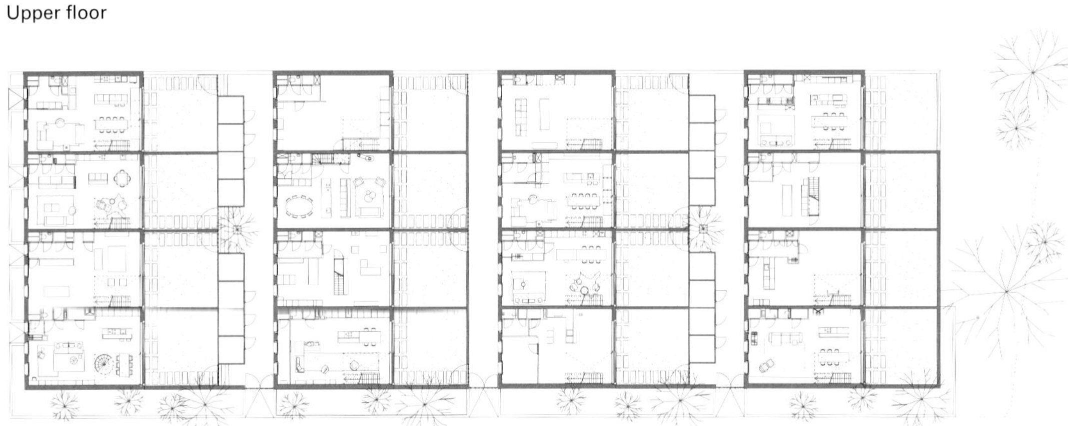

Ground floor

The brick façade and garden wall directly blend into each other.

In contrast to the north façades, the south façades are completely glazed.

Boarding School at the Bella Vista Agronomy Campus in Bolivia

Ralf Pasel

PROJECT NAME
Boarding School at the Bella Vista Agronomy Campus in Bolivia

ARCHITECT/S
CODE | Chair for Construction + Design, Technical University Berlin; Berlin/Germany

BUILDING PURPOSE
Residential housing

LOCATION
Cochabamba, Bolivia

CONSTRUCTION PERIOD
2017

BRICK TYPE
Handmade bricks

BRICK AWARD CATEGORY
Living together

Under the direction of Professor Ralf Pasel, the Department of Structural Design and Construction of the Technical University of Berlin (CODE) has undertaken a long-term project in the Bolivian Andes: In the village of Bella Vista, at an altitude of 2800 meters, the Agronomy Campus with a boarding school was built. The aim of the project is to fight poverty locally, but also to develop solutions to global problems such as increasing urbanization and rural depopulation.

Together with the non-profit organization Cristo Vive Bolivia, students of the Department of Architecture at TU Berlin designed the Agronomy Campus. It was realized in cooperation with local partners and the local population. The Campus is a showcase that offers young people from poorer families a future perspective and at the same time serves as an innovation center for organic farming. Beyond that, the buildings are prototypes designed to have a supra-regional effect.

The boarding house is located at the southeastern end of the area. Its structure makes reference to the landscape and mediates between public spaces, interiors and places of retreat. Featuring large glass doors, the common room opens to the surrounding fields and offers views of the 5000-meter-high Tunari mountain range. In addition to a long dining table, it contains niches built into the walls with work desks, shelves and cupboards. Situated on the north side is a walled patio. On the south side, five sanitary cells separate the common room from the kitchen and the five bedrooms with two to four beds each. All of the bedrooms have access to another elongated, enclosed patio that serves as a quiet place for the students.

> "Regional solutions of global significance"

Architecturally, the boarding house resembles the earlier built agricultural school, because like this structure, it has a large shed roof with strip windows to the south. The floors, walls and the roof construction are made of a separate material: concrete, masonry and wood. Since large temperature differences between day and night prevail in this region of the Andes, a monolithic construction with 29-centimeter-thick walls made up of 80,000 locally handcrafted bricks was chosen. To enable the building to store as much solar heat as possible during the day, it opens mainly to the north. Battening in front of the windows serves as sun breakers. When the students come home from work in the field in the evening, the house radiates the stored heat and provides comfort—without much technical or financial effort. [ab]

The houses of the Agronomie-Campus follow the course of the slope; the dormitory is located at the southern end.

The kitchen lies on the same axis as the bedrooms.

Looking out from the common room to a quiet patio or far across the countryside

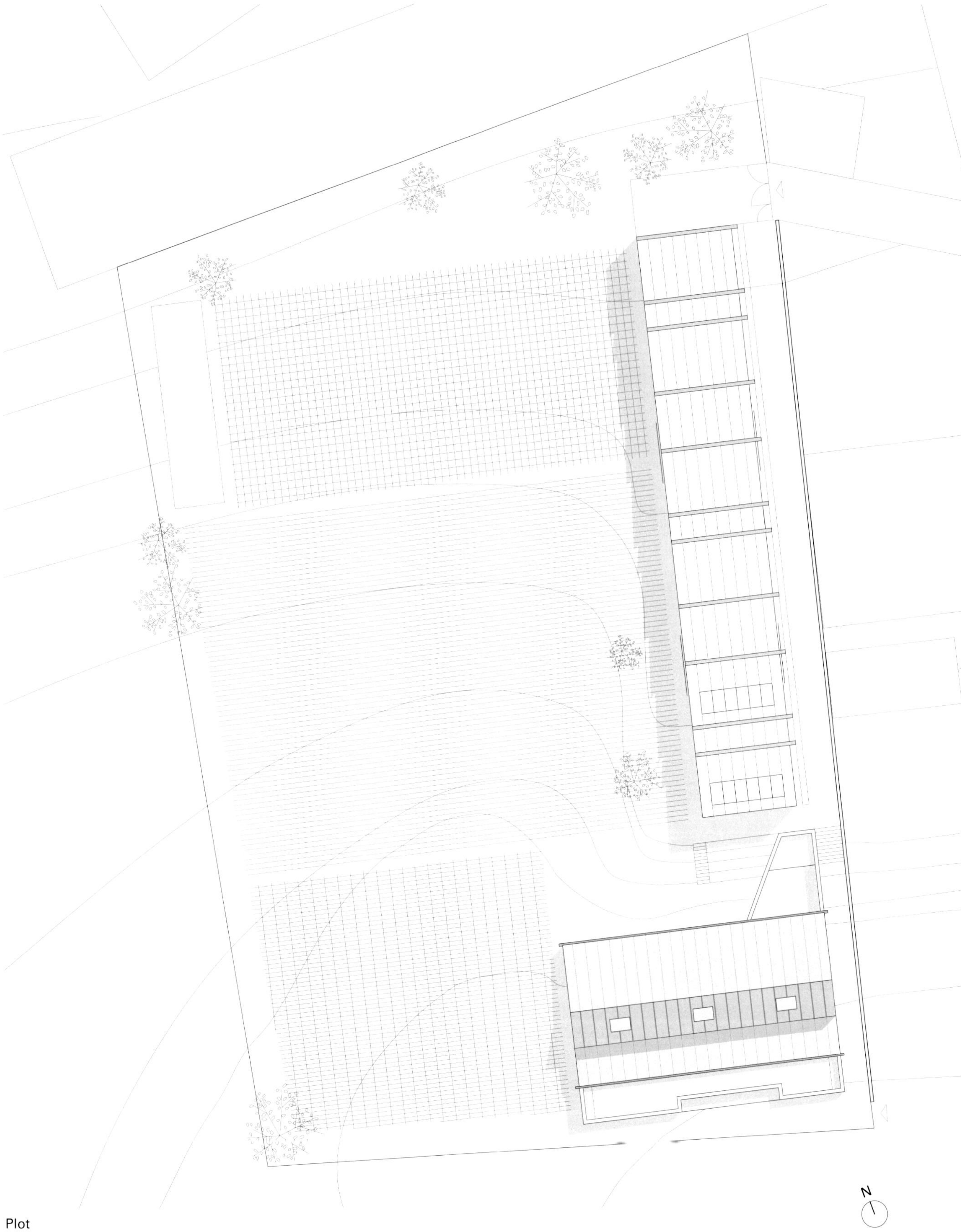

Plot

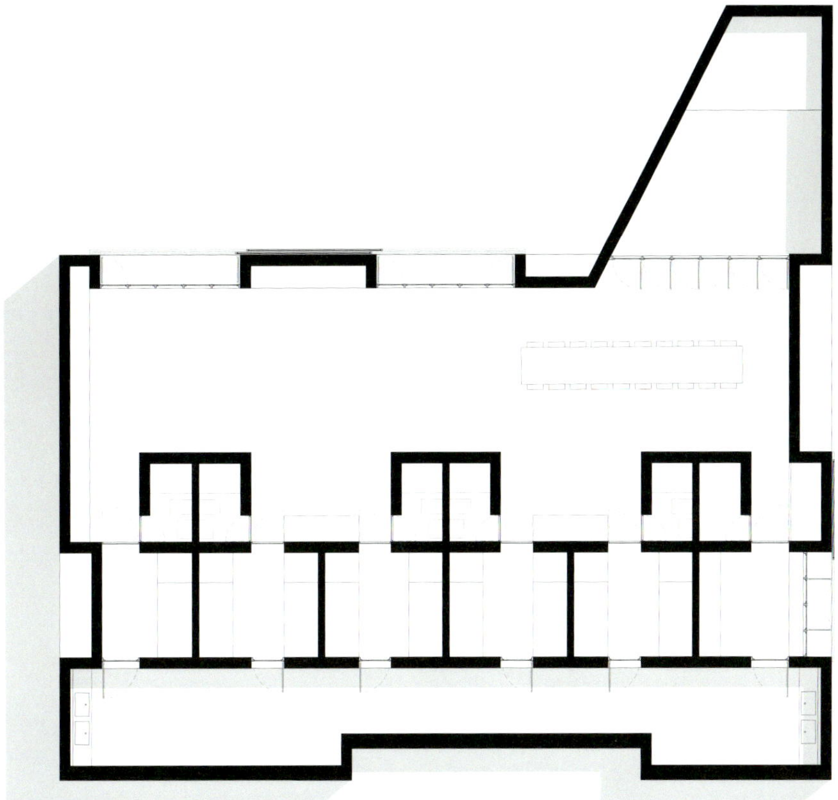

Floor plan

A quiet courtyard area is located in front of the south façade.

A light metal frame provides privacy and protection against the sun.

DMVA ARCHITECTS

Site Apostolinnen

David Driesen and Tom Verschueren

PROJECT NAME
Site Apostolinnen

ARCHITECT/S
dmvA architects,
Mechelen / Belgium

BUILDING PURPOSE
Apartment housing

LOCATION
Mechelen, Belgium

CONSTRUCTION PERIOD
2018

BRICK TYPE
Facing bricks

BRICK AWARD CATEGORY
Living together

Up into the late 18th century, the Apostolines compound in the old town of Mechelen housed a convent. Later, apartments were built and the complex was converted and expanded several times for this purpose, until a mattress factory eventually moved there in 1926. A number of years ago, the mattress manufacturer, who still owns the site, decided to return it to the city as a residential area.

"A combination between new building, renovation and restoration"

At first, the aim of the design was to bring back the missing genius loci. Among other things, it was important to open the area, which had been built up and sealed off over time. Historical research had shown that the complex used to criss-cross several streets which had been built over through the centuries. The reintroduction of the lanes not only spurred on the development of the area, but also made the historic buildings recognizable again as separate volumes.

The old convent wall still runs around the area, but now has doors that open to the street. In the middle of the courtyard stands the so-called summer house from the 17th century, which has been turned into a private residence. In the 20th century it was complemented by a small workers' house, which is now situated in the garden of the summer house and serves as a guesthouse. Next to it is a large 18th-century warehouse containing eight student studios. In the north, the area is bordered by two 19th-century houses, with ground-floor commercial premises facing the street. The architects added six new apartments above them.

However, an idiosyncratic 18th-century bay house and an adjacent new structure with two pitched roofs make up heart of the Apostolines area. Accommodating two triplexes, the new building's bright red brick façades clearly distinguish it from the whitewashed existing stock. Not only are the façades made of the same stretcher-bonded brick, but the external stairs, sleepers, lintels and reveals as well. Weeping mortar joints give the building a strong surface feel and a modern roughness, which forms a contrast to the village-sized scale of the project. The only other material is the black metal of the window frames, which was also used in the other houses for all visible new elements—such as entrance doors and vestibules.

The new structure serves as a catalyst for the entire building complex, as the external staircases that wind around the monolith form a continuation of the semi-public lanes and open the upper floor apartments with the shops. The cross-pollination between old and new has created a fine-grained, rural enclave in the city, which is homey, but thanks to the modern design vocabulary and the contrasting material use does not seem dainty. [ab]

Original access routes were reactivated.

Two new houses with red façades on the left; a restored exisiting building with a white façade on the right.

Axonometry

Passage between the private residence and the old monastery wall

HOUSE OF ARCHITECTS

Tiny Towers

Geurt Holdijk and Guus Peters

PROJECT NAME Tiny Towers	LOCATION Almere, The Netherlands
ARCHITECT/S HOUSE OF ARCHITECTS, Amsterdam/ The Netherlands	CONSTRUCTION PERIOD 2018–2019
BUILDING PURPOSE Apartment housing	BRICK TYPE Facing bricks
	BRICK AWARD CATEGORY Living together

"Het kan in Almere" ("It is possible in Almere") is the slogan of the Dutch polder city. Founded in 1977 on artificial land, Almere quickly gained the reputation of being an experimental field for architecture and urban planning. The Tiny Housing Building Expo, which started in 2016 in the new self-built district of Homeruskwartier, also fits into this picture.

Located in the center of the circularly laid-out district, the building expo site reminds one of a campground at first glance: Caravan creations, wooden huts and A-frame houses romp about on the green lawn. All of them arose from a competition in which sustainable and innovative house designs with less than 50 square meters of living space could be submitted. Prototypes for a possible later mass production were also allowed. Among the 245 entries, the jury selected 25 winners, of which 13 were ultimately realized.

This includes the Tiny Towers. They are intended as a new typology for the often quite uniform Dutch terraced housing estates, which Almere mostly consists of, too. The end lot of a house row could respectively be reserved for such a Tiny Tower, which is composed of three minimal row houses. New groups of residents such as students, seniors or singles could be addressed, thereby contributing to the user heterogeneity of the otherwise family-dominated terraced housing district.

The individual turrets each have a floor area of only 16.7 square meters and extend over three floors and functional areas: kitchen on the ground floor, living room on the first floor, bedroom and bathroom on the second floor, accessed by stairs that are also quite steep by Dutch standards. Each unit has a separate entrance door, as well as a roof terrace.

> "To enlarge the interior and create shadows on the façade, the brick is placed on its side."

Windows and doors all have the same format: a fixed glazed window, and next to it a two-part black door or a black panel with folding shutters. Made of prefabricated concrete elements, the construction was clad with normal-sized, handmade bricks crafted in Germany in the color "Rheinisch Bunt." They were laid sideways, so that the façades were particularly thin and space-saving. Above a one-meter-high base zone, the recesses of the bricks are turned outwards, so that, depending on the position of the sun, a lively relief effect is created on the walls.

Tiny houses are a trend often smirked at—and some of the micro-architecture on the meadow in Almere indeed cannot be taken so seriously. However, the Tiny Towers convince people with their sculptural quality and their pragmatic concept, which could actually be used in many a terraced house district. [ab]

The Tiny Towers are the results of a tiny house building exhibition.

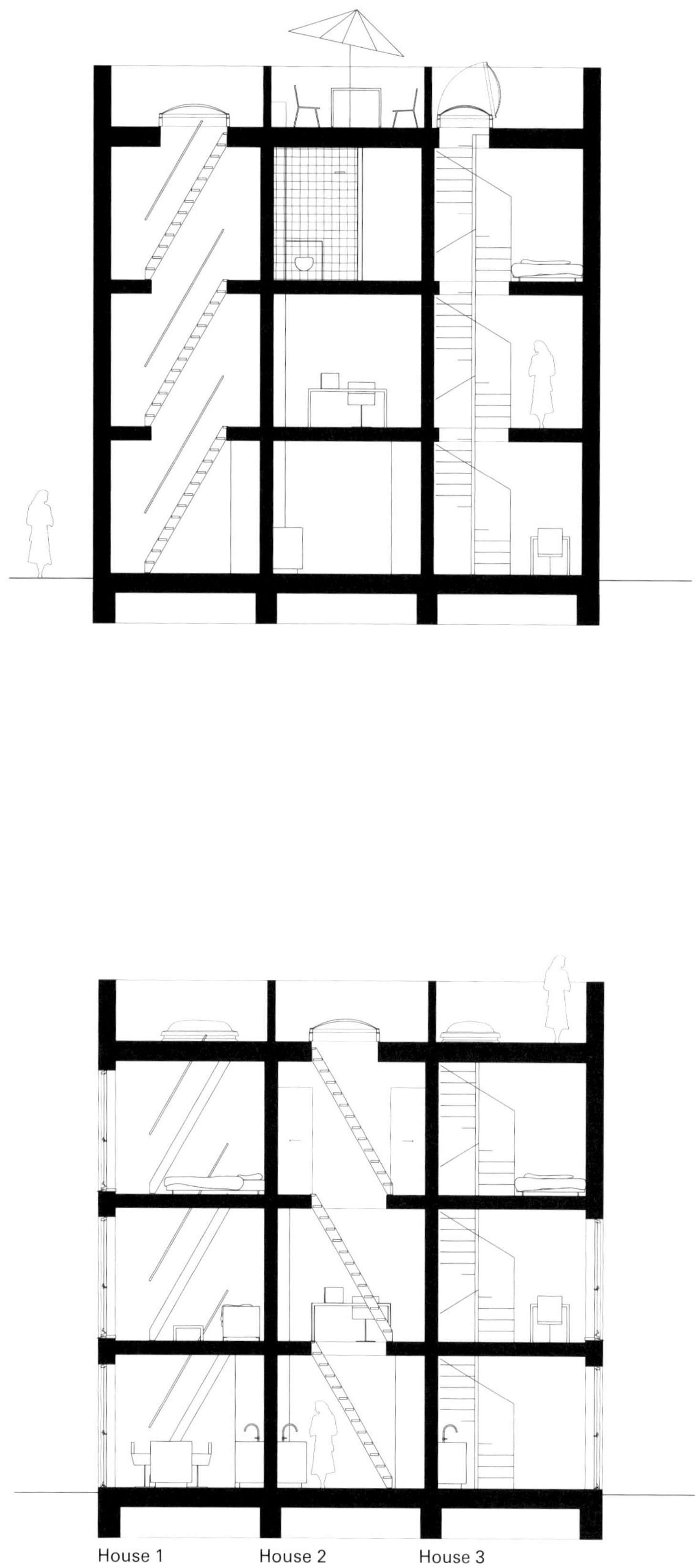

Longitudinal sections through the building

Floor plans

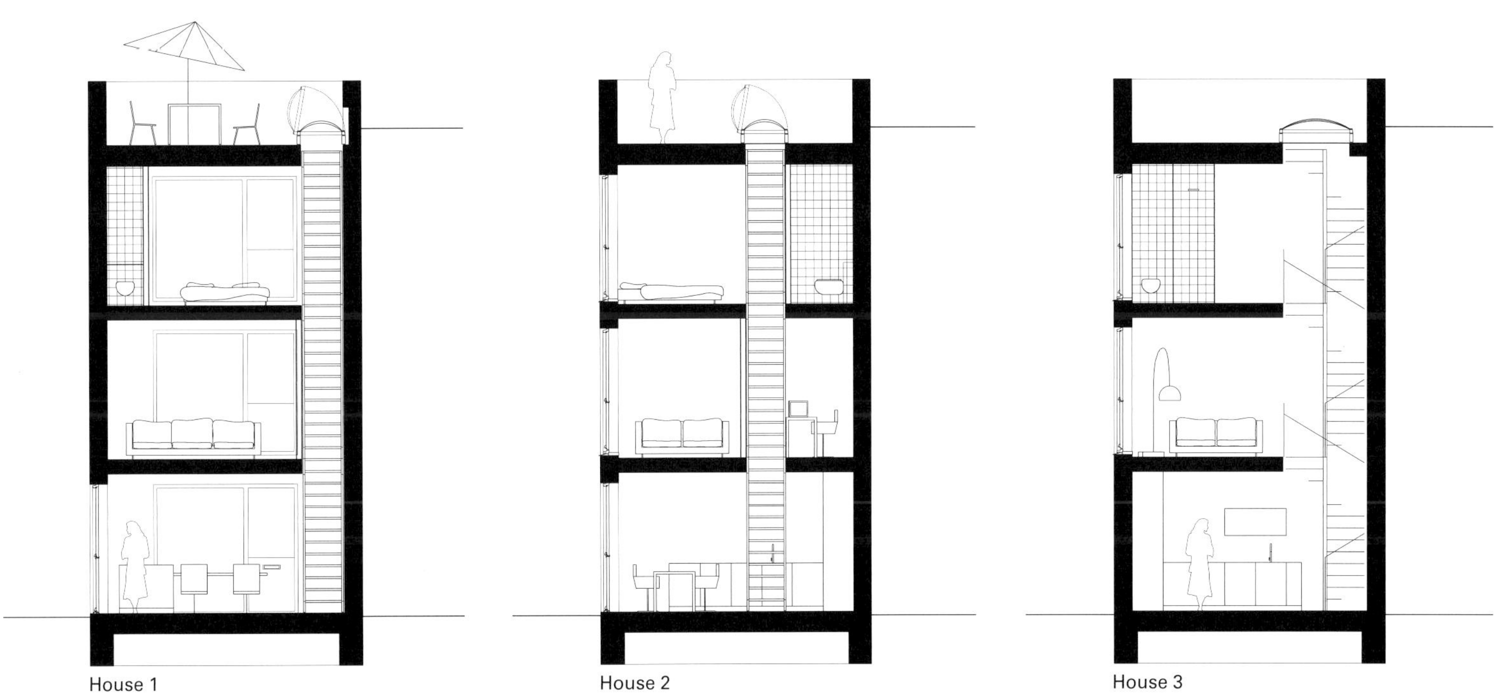

Longitudinal sections through one house respectively

ATELIER DO CARDOSO

Casa Acreditar Porto

João Gomes Leitão and Mafalda Ribeiro Ambrósio

PROJECT NAME
Casa Acreditar Porto

ARCHITECT/S
atelier do cardoso, Lisboa / Portugal

BUILDING PURPOSE
Residential housing

LOCATION
Porto, Portugal

CONSTRUCTION PERIOD
2016

BRICK TYPE
Ceramic façade panels

BRICK AWARD CATEGORY
Living together

Casa Acreditar in Porto is a residential home where children and adolescents with cancer can live with their families while they are being treated at the nearby hospital. As a result of an architectural competition, the design of the Lisbon-based atelier do cardoso was implemented, financed exclusively by donations and grants from sponsors.

The house is pushed into a slope, so that the two-story base area lies partially in the ground, surrounding it like a protective wall. In this gray granite-clad foundation, spaces for visitors, staff and volunteers were set up in the lower level, above which the common areas are located — kitchens, laundry, living and dining rooms. Areas for the younger children and the adolescents that can be read as interconnected cubes rise above the plinth. 16 rooms with two beds, a bathroom and one common room for both age groups are accommodated in them.

The structure was developed according to the principle of subtractive volumes: Blocks were removed on all sides of the imaginary total body that results when the rectangle circumscribing the base is raised, leading to the figure that was finally built: a compact volume with incisions that ensure all the rooms are well-lit and that a small courtyard on the ground floor and a terrace on the first floor could find space.

> "The main objective of this project was to create a building, a living space with the maximum of comfort, that could help to overcome the longing, creating a familiar environment in a coexistence."

This design principle was also used for the outer surfaces: All surfaces lying outside the imaginary total volume are plastered white. Those that result through the incisions are clad in soft green tiles — as if you were looking at the intersecting planes of the interior. Lending the house a bright, clear effect, the soft green color was developed especially for this project. With the tiles, called azulejos in Portugal, a typical and traditional element in Porto was additionally used, one which had also been applied during the Modernist period — for example, by Álvaro Siza and Eduardo Souto de Moura — as a matter of course.

Arranged in a regular grid, the 14 × 14 centimeter terracotta tiles can also be found inside: in the kitchens, stairwells and bathrooms. Iridescent shades and slight irregularities that make the surfaces pleasantly alive were created through hand finishing. In the interior, the range of colors was extended by more hues: built-in furniture and bathroom tiles are partly in a strong red and there are parquet floors and ceiling sound elements made of wood material, so that a warm, homey atmosphere has arisen, one which the children and young people need to be in to make them feel secure at a time that is so difficult for them. [ch]

The courtyard walls are also clad with the bright green brick tiles.

Site plan

The building shape arose according to the principle of subtractive volumes.

Edificio Damero

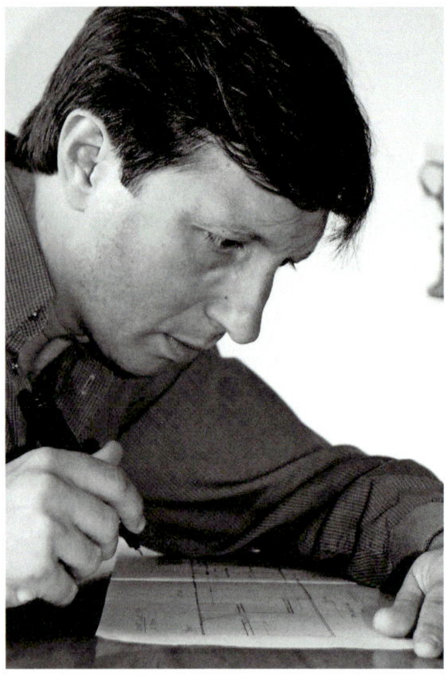

Francisco Cadau

PROJECT NAME	LOCATION
Edificio Damero	Campana, Argentina
ARCHITECT/S	CONSTRUCTION PERIOD
Francisco Cadau Oficina de Arquitectura, Campana/Argentina	2017–2019
	BRICK TYPE
	Clay blocks
BUILDING PURPOSE	BRICK AWARD CATEGORY
Apartment housing	Living together

Solid is the first word that comes to mind with the Edificio Damero. As the only higher building, the brick monolith soars above a low-rise, mixed development block in the town of Campana near Buenos Aires. The five-story edifice houses a total of 20 apartments. Their loggias afford views of a green area across the street and the gardens in the interior of the block.

On the ground floor level, the property is almost completely overbuilt. Facing the street side, the lobby is adjoined by a semi-recessed parking garage with a parking deck in the rear. Above this rises the elevated cube, which reacts to its surroundings by means of slants and loggias. The building was therefore moved a little out of the street line so that a pine tree could be preserved as part of the new front yard. A round recess for an old avocado tree is on the parking deck.

> "The project is developed from the textures and permeability of the brick skin."

Access to the building is provided on the north side. The volume is slightly slanted there to create distance to the neighboring structure. On each floor there are four apartments in a central corridor: three smaller lofts and one larger one on the first, third and fifth floors; three small lofts and a three-room apartment on the second and fourth floors. Each apartment has a loggia that faces either eastward or westward; diagonally opposite is a core with a bathroom and kitchen. This division creates a checkerboard pattern on the two main façades: loggias, closed façade surfaces and open masonry, which serves as a brise soleil in front of the windows, alternate with each other. The building is completed by a slanted roof edge, which reminds one somewhat of a mansard roof.

The construction is made of reinforced concrete, around which a skin of red-orange bricks with mica aggregate lays. The 24 × 11 × 5 centimeter bricks are laid in a stretcher bond. In front of the window openings, however, the stretchers are rotated in seven steps around their own axis until they become headers that protrude out of the façade at a 90-degree angle. Bricks are laid openly in the side façades and in front of the extra-large loggias on the north face of the second and fourth floors. The stretchers were not rotated there, but rather walled up in the gap. Two projecting, slit-shaped openings per floor in the south façade offer an additional light source for the apartments.

As massive as the monolith may seem at first glance, it is nonetheless cleverly modeled into its hybrid context and plays with openness and closure, geometry and sculpture, surface and relief. [ab]

Open loggias as well as pierced and closed masonry structure the surfaces of the residence.

The east façade viewed from the green space of a school.

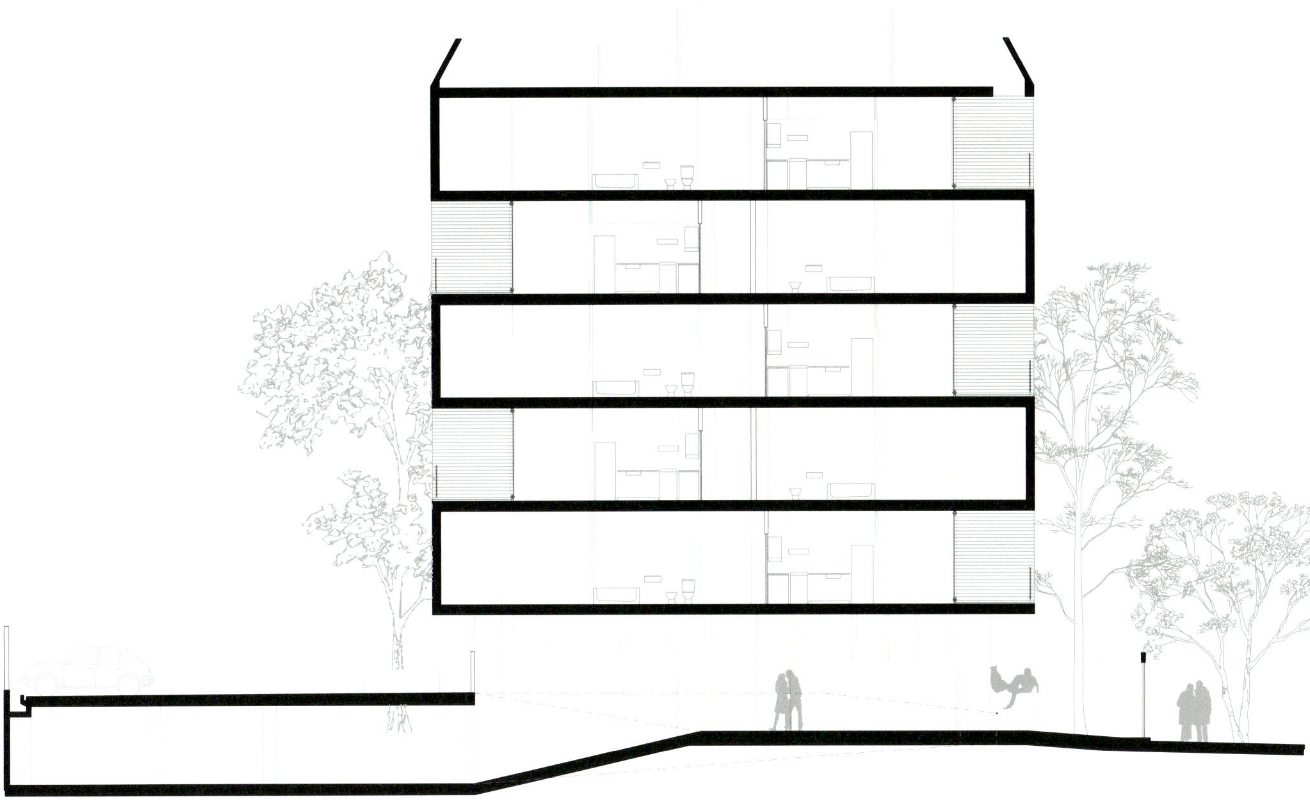

Section

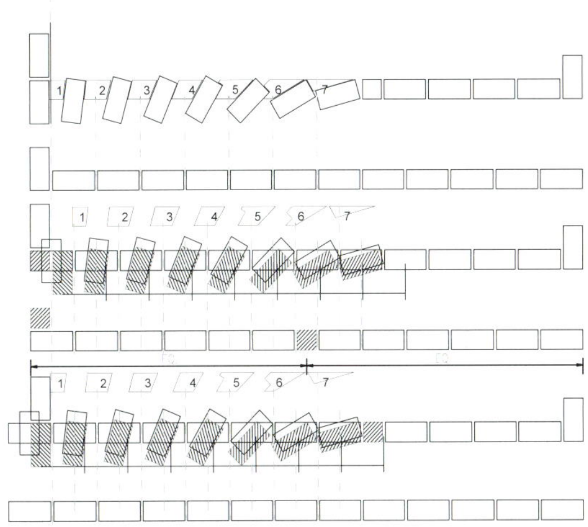

Brick scheme

DBG – D'HONDT BEYENS GOESAERT

Youth Nursing Home De Hoge Kouter

Bruno D'hondt, Dries Goesaert and Xavier Beyens

PROJECT NAME
Youth Nursing Home De Hoge Kouter

ARCHITECT/S
Architecten- en Ingenieursbureau D'hondt Beyens Goesaert, Kortrijk/Belgium

BUILDING PURPOSE
Residential housing

LOCATION
Kortrijk, Belgium

CONSTRUCTION PERIOD
2018–2019

BRICK TYPE
Clay blocks, facing bricks

BRICK AWARD CATEGORY
Living together

From the end of the 13th century, Kortrijk, among other towns and cities in Flanders, produced impressive buildings—secular and ecclesiastical—in new-found brick. Rapidly growing settlements with large and dense populations needed a variety of new buildings. Brick allowed these to be realized quickly. Flemish brickwork was to become expert, innovative and, in the right hands, beautiful. With particular buildings, brick could also be comforting, a homey material worked by human hands.

> "The bricks act as a map for those who can't orientate well, but can feel and remember."

It seems appropriate then that the new De Hoge Kouter (Catholic Orthopedagogic Center Kortrijk), a residential school for young people with mental or physical disabilities, should be designed in the guise of a sequence of friendly brick houses. Facing a street on one side and a park on the other, this is an institutional building with a notably cozy feel. In creating this atmosphere, D'hondt Beyens Goesaert have shaped a building that might seem at first sight to be a cluster of independent gabled brick houses, but is in fact all of a piece. In breaking down elevations and façades into homey forms, and with separate entrances leading, ultimately, into communal spaces, the building has a gently varied presence. It has, say its architects, "the atmosphere of four small scaled houses, but the functionality of one rational organization."

Residential dayrooms and bedrooms face the public park while rooms for visitors, counseling and therapy face the street. The importance of this architectural project is that it normalizes a specialist care center. This is a high quality yet everyday building that fits comfortably into its residential and parkland setting. The low-key massing of the building together with the architects' choice of brick as a building material are factors that have worked seamlessly to shape a comfortable place to be.

"This is not a facility or a boarding hostel," say the architects. "This is home, created with warm, red bricks with a tactile, playful texture. The texture of the brick walls also has another function: Not every wall has an incorporated pattern. The combination of the textured walls and the simple brick walls guides the children to their own living area. It functions as a map for those who can't orientate well, but can feel and remember." [jg]

The complex conveys the intimacy of gabled-topped brick houses.

Different textures facilitate orientation – also on the haptic level.

Through the comprehensible scalability the children's home blends in well with the surroundings and the kids can find their way easily around the premises.

Project ERC

Matias Madsen and Cristian Larraín

PROJECT NAME
Project ERC

ARCHITECT/S
MAPAA,
Providencia / Chile

BUILDING PURPOSE
Apartment housing

LOCATION
Santiago, Chile

CONSTRUCTION PERIOD
2016–2017

BRICK TYPE
Facing bricks

BRICK AWARD CATEGORY
Living together

Providencia is a city in the metropolitan area of Santiago de Chile. In the context of a development from the 1940s, an approximately thirty-year-old residential building stood empty before it was renovated and revitalized according to a plan by the architects MAPAA. It consists of a front and a rear building. Located between these two parts is the stairwell that connects them.

"ERC is an apartment building which uses hand-made trapezoidal brick veneer."

During the renovation, the architects faced two important questions: Firstly, the house was supposed to show that it had been altered without denying the context of the neighboring buildings. Erected quite uniformly and coherently almost 80 years ago, the house had not changed much since then. On the other hand, the lighting was to be improved. The answers to both of these questions are to be found in the façade.

Reminiscent of the formal repertoire of a Gründerzeit development, the conventional existing buildings are of a subdued color; their quality lies in a modeled structure with many variants. To incorporate, but not to imitate this, the architects added a facing shell of prefabricated elements, with red, hand-crafted clay bricks, to their object. They abandoned the classical principles of window framing and base and parapet formation that characterize the neighboring buildings, but used a structure otherwise animated by light and shadow: The conventional brick formats were cut to give each brick four trapezoidal parts, which were lined up in sawtooth manner. The direction of the sawtooth alternated each layer, resulting in the nearly textile-like structure of the façade. An L-shaped framing of smoothly laid bricks communicates to the adjacent, higher building.

To bring more light into the spaces, new, larger windows set with dark steel frames were used. They consist of a deep, narrow opening wing and a façade-flush fixed glazing that almost reaches the floor of the story. These prefabricated window elements likewise help to stabilize the new wall structure, but also shape the character of the renovated house, which now oscillates between industrial construction, serial structure and hand-crafted expression, bridging the past and the present.

The total of seven apartments can be divided into two types: an approximately 35-square-meter-large studio and an 80-square-meter, two-room apartment, each uniformly fitted with parquet floors, white walls and white tiles in the kitchen and sanitary area. In both cases, the architects opt for an open-plan form of living, so that the benefits of the larger windows and the better lighting are actually shown off to their advantage. [ch]

127

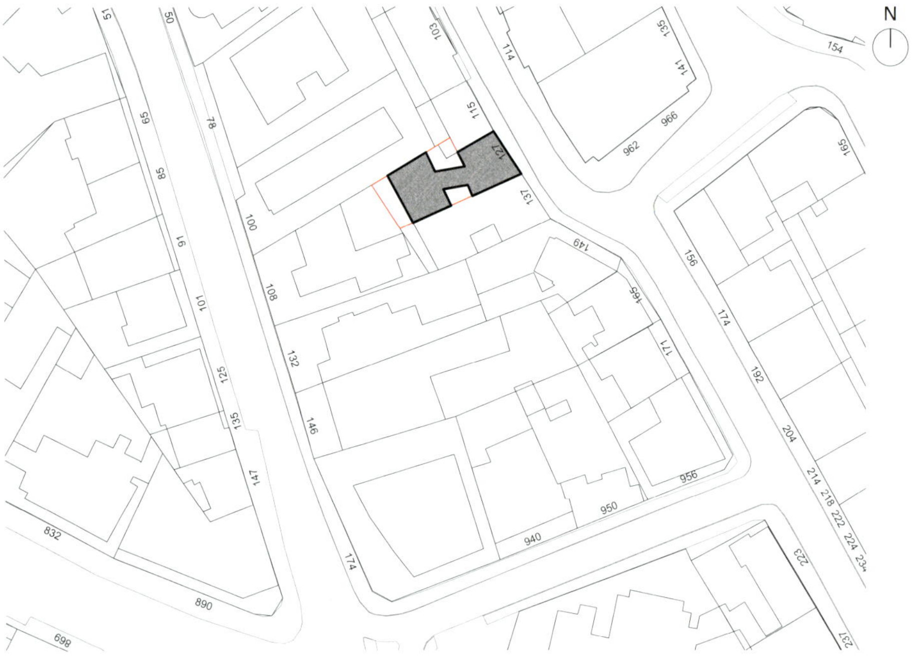

Site plan

A white plastered façade covers the rear part of the building, large window openings and the structured brick façade dominate on the street side.

A facing shell made of prefabricated brick elements was placed in front of the existing façade.

Working together

LAURA ILONIEMI

The Workplace Metamorphosis of Brick

Laura Iloniemi

Our working culture is in flux. Many employers are reinterpreting the idea of the corporate office, both in terms of leadership strategy and the design and feel of workplaces. The less-hierarchical nature of the open plan office has played an important role in this shift, but with digitalization, other new concerns have been introduced.

Open plan or not, a reoccurring phenomenon in contemporary workplaces is that of near silent floors of desks. This holds true particularly in architects' studios where staff, whether in Helsinki, London or New York, wear headphones while working. Headphones or not, people tend to be so glued to their screens that during their working day they are increasingly unaware of one another and so much so that some architects organize separate pin-up sessions so that colleagues have some familiarity with each other's projects.

It is interesting to note how, in this somewhat insular and even alienating context, the physical materiality of workplace interiors has come to play such an important role. There is a hankering after something that expresses a sense of craft, of creating or making something even though white-collar workers are entirely removed from the realm of manual labor. This longing for physical production in increasingly digitalized workplaces has coincided with the popularity of semi-industrial brick warehouses and workshops. Whether new or old, such building types and, more generally, architecture inspired by such functional, factory-like settings are what we now covet, and are what developers have learned to celebrate in their schemes. Even letting agents have caught onto this by celebrating the notion of industrial chic offices much as they did with rise of the 1980s loft apartment fad.

The truth is that this trend for the exposed brick wall office look speaks of another era, of economies reliant on manufacturing. It is therefore fair to say that with it comes a degree of nostalgia for the days when our local communities still made physical things. This is compounded with a heightened need to feel a sense of place or for some tactile association with one's environment, one that gives us comfort when so much of today's trade is service-based and easily disappears into the ether. In this sense, the earthiness of bricks feels both sensual and solid, or haptic as architects like to say. Haptic because bricks are tactile and play to our sense of memory.

> "This longing for physical production in increasingly digitalized workplaces has coincided with the popularity of semi-industrial brick warehouses and workshops."

Modern architects have, of course, used brick in office buildings in imaginative ways that are not just about imbuing workplaces with a sense of "labor as craft" or with labor rooted in the genius loci created by so many 19th century brick workshops, factories, and even industrial estates. For example, there are poetic interpretations of brick that are exemplary of the gravitas and timelessness of great Modernist architecture. Consider the work of Alvar Aalto (1898–1976) and, especially, Säynätsalo Town Hall (1952) or his Helsinki projects, like the National Pensions Institute (1957), the House of Culture (1957) and the University of Technology in Otaniemi (1966) just outside the capital (now called Aalto University). And there are, of course, other architects working in this period whose names are associated with brick masterpieces. Louis Kahn (1901–1974) comes to mind easily and particularly his project for the Indian Institute of Management in Ahmedabad (1974). It is fascinating to observe how brick, although a commonplace material, in the hands of such pioneering architects does lend itself beautifully to achieving a highly moving artistic form—and even in the context of administrative or office architecture.

Thinking of the artistic potential of brick, there are delightful recent examples of architects working with brick masonry to create arches, bas-reliefs or patterns that play with light and shadow. Perforated brick structures are a visually compelling example of this potential and, as a result, have been capturing the imaginations of many on social media, as well as editors working on design publications. Federico Marinaro Architect's "Little Building" in Rosario Argentina (2017) is a very subtle take on this theme. Interestingly, his perforated brick wall is also about adding a sense of privacy and sun protection in the workplace, an approach no doubt welcomed by those all too familiar with the problems of being exposed while working in glass towers and suffering from glare and heat gain.

In addition to their functional qualities, such details can also play an important part in raising the architectural quality of office buildings in ways that make these feel more civic and thereby worthy neighbors to public buildings. This is perhaps why conservation architects and heritage experts often welcome the use of brick in urban areas. It is also a material that ages well. It is inspiring to see new offices that bridge tradition and innovation in terms of how they use brick in an original way, as exemplified by The Old Post Office project in the center of Hamburg (2018) by Tchoban Voss Architekten. Such buildings often feel grounded, yet also contemporary in much the same way a good enterprise should.

> "It is inspiring to see new offices that bridge tradition and innovation in terms of how they use brick in an original way."

The use of custom designed bricks and flush mortars has yielded exciting results in brick architecture playing on the material's texture and creating more abstracted buildings that are not unlike sculpted objects. Casper Mueller Kneer Architects' project for Céline in Seoul (2017) is a strong example of this type of approach. Perhaps the combination of offices with high fashion retail has pushed this brief into a distinctly artful interpretation of a workplace building. The result is an office block that looks like an arts foundation or gallery. It plays on the duality of brick as a material that extends from its humble blue collar worlds described above to vogue catwalk worlds represented by Céline.

OFFICE WINHOV & GOTTLIEB PALUDAN ARCHITECTS

City Archive Delft

Jan Peter Wingender and Jesper Gottlieb

PROJECT NAME
City Archive Delft

ARCHITECT/S
Office Winhov (Amsterdam/The Netherlands) & Gottlieb Paludan Architects (Copenhagen/Denmark)

BUILDING PURPOSE
Offices, archive

LOCATION
Delft, The Netherlands

CONSTRUCTION PERIOD
2016–2017

BRICK TYPE
Facing bricks

BRICK AWARD CATEGORY
Working together

BRICK 20 Category Winner

The Delft City Archive is a repository of knowledge, a treasure chamber and a place of study at the same time. It has the somewhat contradictory task of protecting valuable documents from external influences while making them accessible to the public. This new building combines these two functions in the form of a huge, abstracted bookshelf.

> "The new Delft City Archive refers to the tradition of brick architecture in the historic center, which gives this important civic building a timeless and robust character."

The City Archive is situated on the edge of a business district in the west of Delft, on the border to the city center. Its structure is divided into two parts: an L-shaped plinth containing the study halls, cafeteria and offices, and above that a closed cube with the archive. In keeping with its public function, the bright concrete base is completely surrounded by story-high window openings. With its bright color, it is reminiscent of the many white-plastered public buildings in the otherwise brick-dominated historic city center of Delft.

A closed cube with apparently five stories rises above. In reality, it contains two depot levels with rows of shelves and, at the top, an additional mezzanine as a technical level. As the archive is located in a polder just below sea level, the elevated position also protects the valuable documents from water damage caused by flooding. With their geometric arrangements, the fully enclosed façades of the archive area make one think of a bookshelf: slender slabs made of prefabricated concrete parts form the "shelves," between which brick pilasters, reminiscent of book spines, protrude at various lengths.

Laid in a stretcher bond with deep joints, the waterstruck bricks were developed by a German clinker manufacturer especially for this construction. Thanks to a coal fire, their color varies from orange to brown, contrasting effectively with the white concrete.

The building presents itself as a tectonic line composition with a depth effect. Not just bookshelves, but also the monochrome reliefs by the Delft artist Jan Schoonhoven served as sources of inspiration. The degree of abstraction of the reliefs meets the haptic qualities of the bricks and creates a sculptural solitaire that is both closed and accessible. [ab]

ARCHIEF

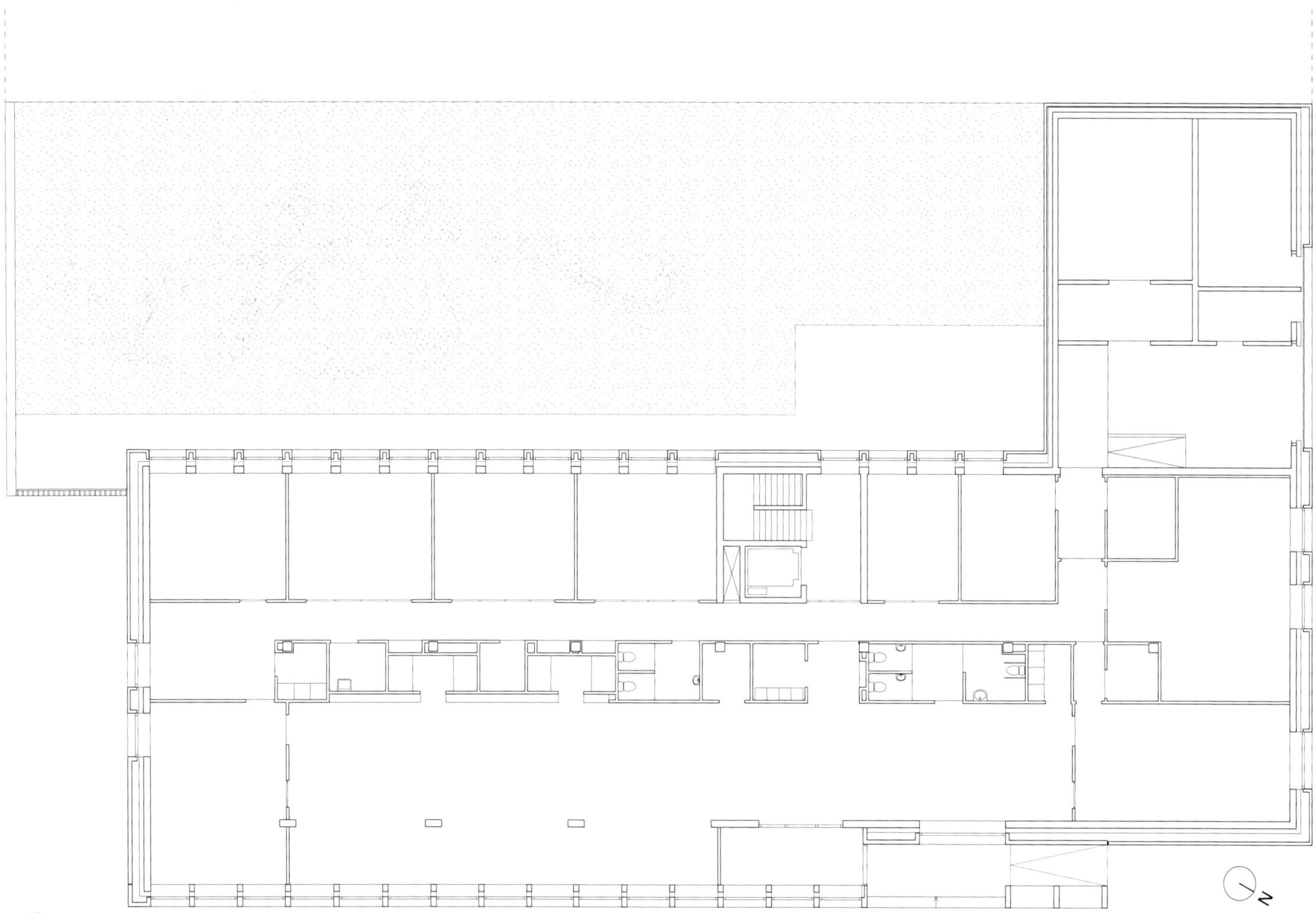

Ground floor

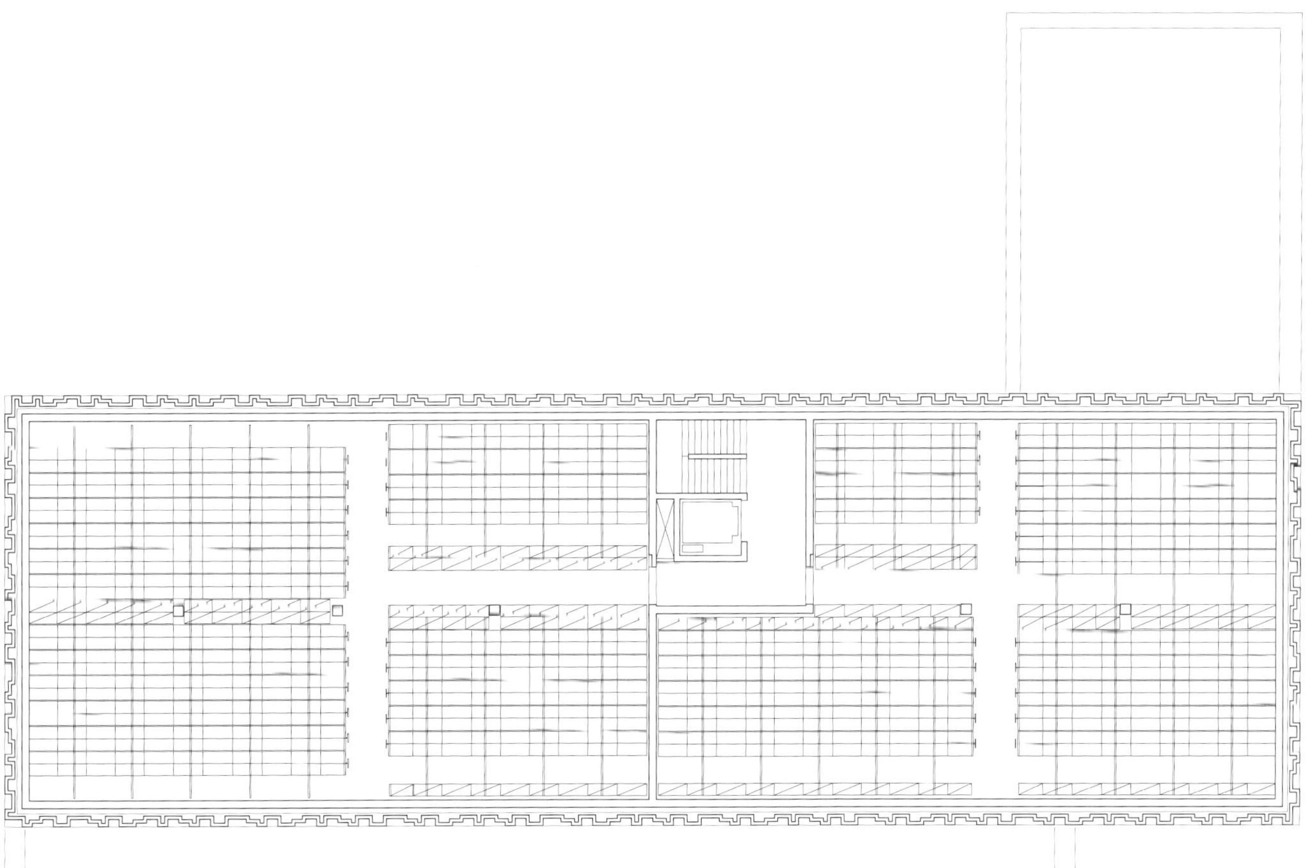

First floor (depot)

Jury statement

"The jury found the project to be conceptually clear and precise. The open ground floor is very much in keeping with the Archive's role as a public building, a place where the history of the city can be displayed and accessed. In contrast, the closed façades of the upper floors enclose the storage facilities of the archive.

The façade of the project is arranged as a series of vertically displaced brick registers, held between concrete horizontals. Great care has been taken to adjust the forward and back plane of the brick surface, and this offers a formal playfulness while evoking the shelving of files and books inside of the building. The jury found the project to be a worthy winner of the 'Working together' category."

The view from the reading room into the park

The horizontal structuring does not correspond to the actual number of two storage floors and a technical level.

ARCHIEF

The façade appears like an oversized bookshelf on all sides.

NKBAK

Stylepark Building at the Churchyard

Nicole Kerstin Berganski and Andreas Krawczyk

PROJECT NAME
Stylepark Building at the Churchyard

ARCHITECT/S
NKBAK, Frankfurt am Main/Germany

BUILDING PURPOSE
Apartment housing, office

LOCATION
Frankfurt am Main, Germany

CONSTRUCTION PERIOD
2017–2019

BRICK TYPE
Facing bricks

BRICK AWARD CATEGORY
Working together

BRICK 20 Honorary Mention

First of all, it is not unusual when a small company operating an Internet portal commissions a new office building and two small apartments in the backyard. The property belongs to the family of the entrepreneur, who had already used office space in the existing building. So far, so good. But what made things a bit more complicated was the circumstance that the listed wall of the neighboring cemetery stands on the back border of the small lot—and this is, after all, the oldest cemetery in Frankfurt. A new building would always be clearly visible here. Given that the cemetery wall, made of sand and bricks and embedded with grave plates, had been extended in the post-war years, planning had to be carried out with care and respect. The architects decided to let the existing wall transition into the outer wall of the annex: The new, therefore, continues the old, just as it used to be in the past, in other places and at other times.

The new building has three stories: the ground floor with the office spaces attaches directly to the old structure; the two upper floors, each taking in a small apartment, have been moved away from it. Each apartment is allotted a small terrace; a further terrace is accessible from the front building. The cubature is structured in such a way that the rules applying to the distance between buildings were taken into account. At the same time, sufficient lighting could be guaranteed for all spaces. In order not to create an atmosphere of confinement, the rooms vary in height and also feature large-sized windows. The offices on the ground floor, which the preservationists only allowed a narrow light slit in the outer wall for, are now illuminated mainly by two inner courtyards, which can also be used as lounges in the summer.

"Bricks are laid onto existing bricks. Logical and easy."

In order not to let the external appearance of the clam-shell brickwork contrast too strongly with the cemetery wall, handmade bricks in three formats (Hamburg, Flensburg and Danish standard format) and in different, but coordinated colors and structures, were used. This ensures that the cemetery wall, with its alternating layers of bricks, does not continue with a uniform and sterile clinker façade in the new building. The windows were darkly framed and thus remain restrained compared to the brickwork. When taking a casual glance, the lively mix of the new brick walls seems happenstance. Upon closer inspection it first becomes clear how much effort the house was planned and detailed with. [ch]

Honorary mention:
"This is a careful exercise in building a new brick structure on a much older masonry foundation, where old and new elements are legible in the façades. This building hosts a mixed program and was appreciated for its poetic qualities and for the sensitive manner in which it adds to an existing place.

The expression of the building is suitably ambigious, blurring any clear reading of its purpose, while its form is bold and distinctive, with a series of loosely placed openings."

The existing wall and the outer wall of the addition transition into each other.

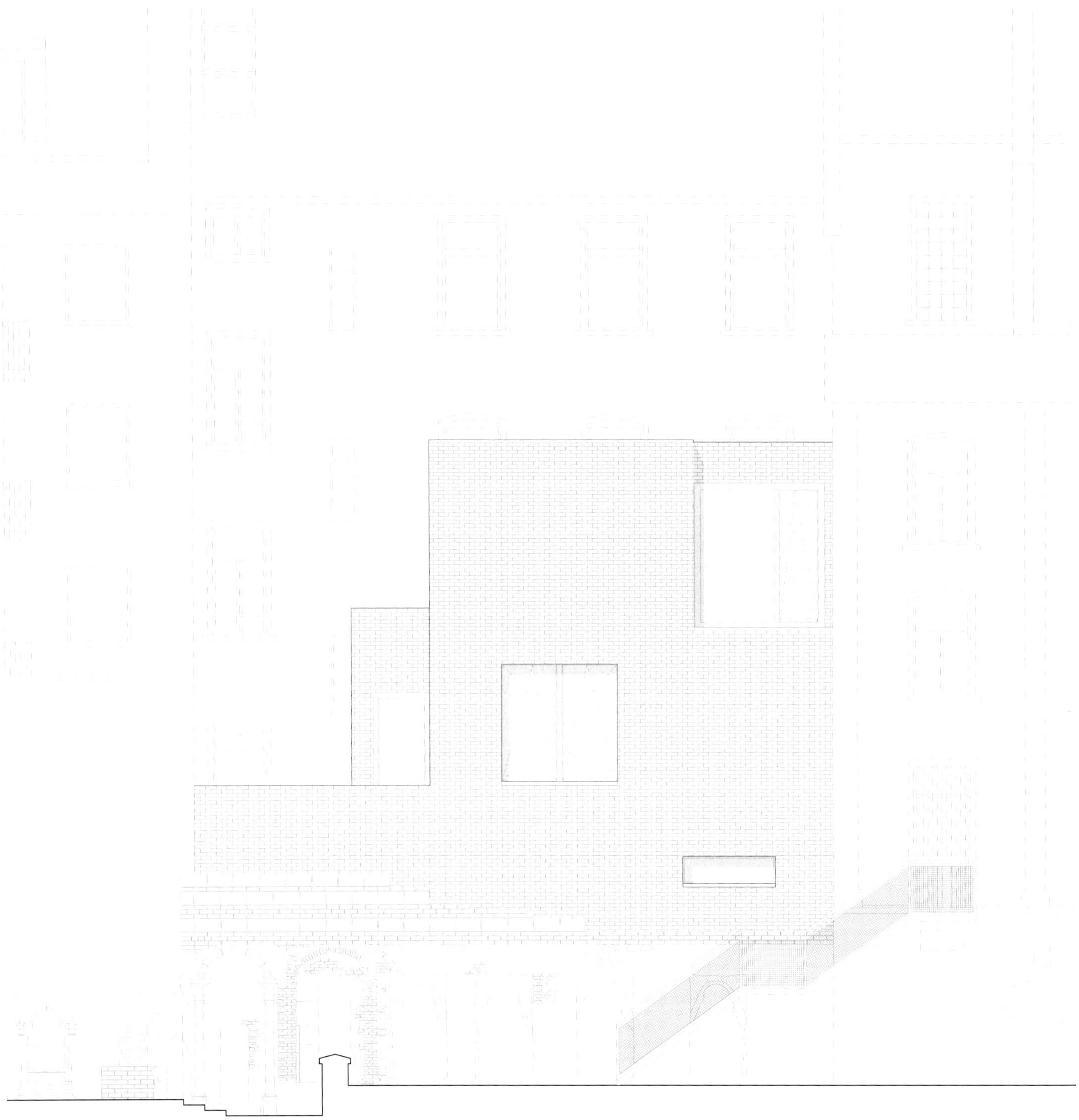

Elevation

The situation before the construction of the addition

Working together

ESTUDIO FEDERICO MARINARO

Little Building

Federico Marinaro

PROJECT NAME
Little Building

ARCHITECT/S
Estudio Federico Marinaro, Rosario/ Argentina

BUILDING PURPOSE
Offices, apartments, practices

LOCATION
Rosario, Argentina

CONSTRUCTION PERIOD
2016–2017

BRICK TYPE
Clay blocks

BRICK AWARD CATEGORY
Working together

In 1852, Rosario, a port on the Paraná River with good access to the Atlantic Ocean, won city status. Newly open to international free trade, the fledgling Argentinean city boomed. Its population, including tides of immigrants from across Europe, soared. Grids of new streets and buildings extended out from its small historic center in a rational if matter-of-fact manner. From politics to architecture, new and progressive ideas from across the Atlantic reached the city. Some of these ideas were positively revolutionary: Rosario was to be the birthplace of Ernesto "Che" Guevara.

Many of the gridded streets rushed up from the mid-19th century in this sub-tropical city have a charm of their own. Vera Mujica is shaded along its slightly ramshackle length by mature plane trees offering welcome shade and greenery. On this street, the Little Building designed by Federico Marinaro with Sofia Settimini can be found, its entrance largely hidden by trees. This is a modest brick building comprising a small number of offices and studio apartments reached from a bright stairwell leading up from the car park underneath and to the back of the compact site. The locally-sourced brickwork exhibits a variety of subtly understated colors from beige to gray and even a gently roseate pink.

Each unit has a balcony facing the street shaded by the plane trees. Finished in elemental materials—concrete, timber and tiles—the are simple, sparse and yet attractive. Squeezed into a tight plot with neighboring buildings on all sides, their privacy is guaranteed by the screen of trees to the street and, to the rear of the building, by a retaining wall punctuated with perforated brick screens. Both screens—arboreal and brick—bring dappled, sub-tropical sunlight into the heart on the inside. This screening is also a way of addressing what is—seen from office windows and the roof terrace—a messy urban setting. The screens act as visual filters.

"The locally-sourced brickwork exhibits a variety of subtly understated colors from beige to gray and even a gently roseate pink."

Here, then, is one exemplary way of building small houses with flexible use, in warm, natural materials, in busy city streets: the units offer a high degree of privacy and the building—a good neighbor in terms of architectural design—is comfortably discreet.

The Little Building is not an expensive proposition and yet it offers a credible alternative to the kind of much larger and highly serviced, high-rise urban offices and apartment complexes that, by their nature, demand open space around them and, all too often, the demolition of the type of modest buildings that constitute Rosario's Vera Mujica. [jg]

The plain units are suitable for different uses.

A view-protected terrace is located on the roof.

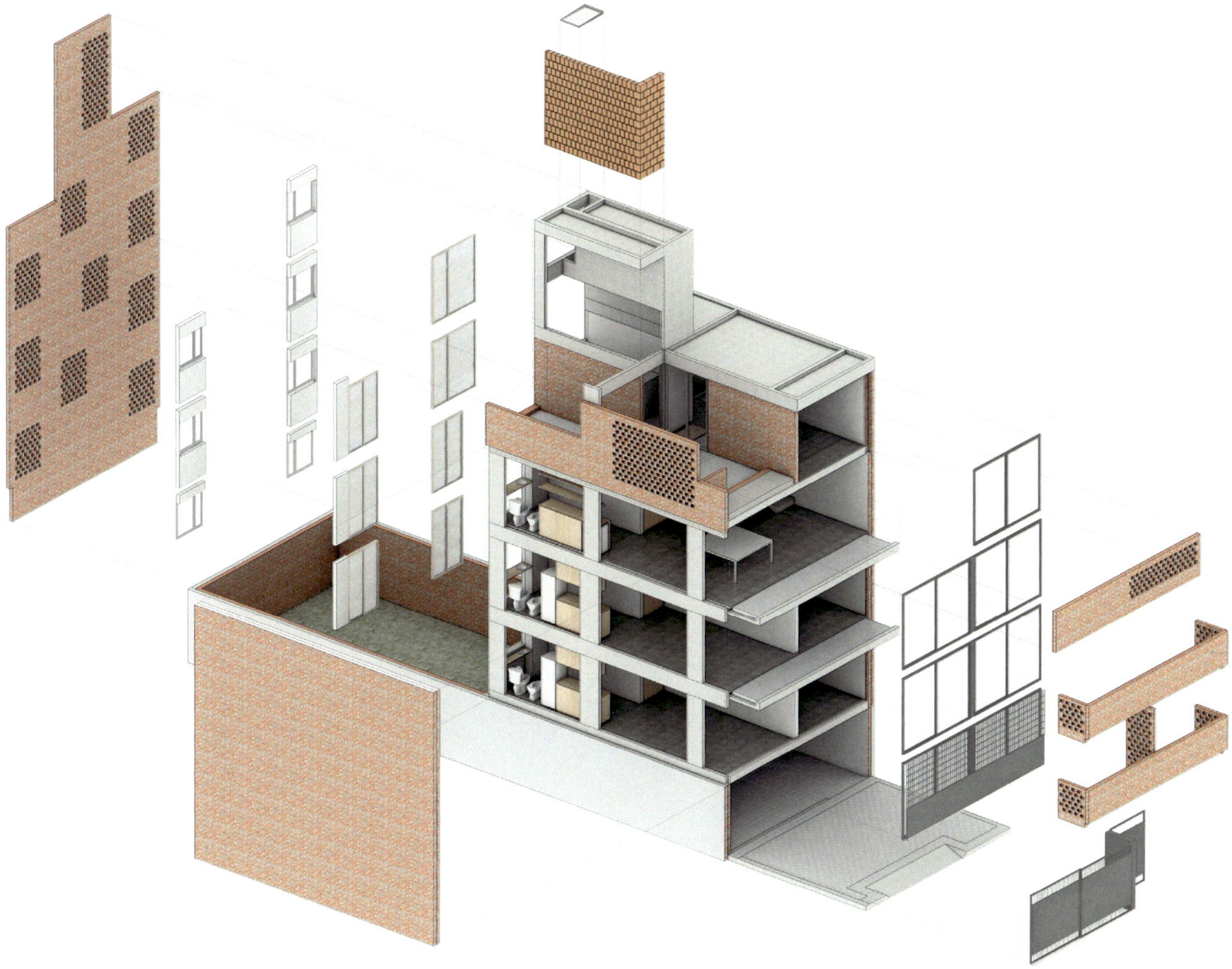

The Little Building fits well into its surrounding in terms of scale, color and materiality.

ANDREAS HEUPEL ARCHITEKTEN BDA

H7

Andreas Heupel

PROJECT NAME	LOCATION
H7	Münster, Germany
ARCHITECT/S	CONSTRUCTION PERIOD
Andreas Heupel Architekten BDA, Münster/Germany	2014–2017
	BRICK TYPE
	Ceramic façade panels
BUILDING PURPOSE	BRICK AWARD CATEGORY
Offices	Working together

Situated on the south bank of the former city harbor of Münster, the H7 Office Building is green through and through—both in terms of its color scheme and its eco-balance. It is currently the tallest wooden hybrid building in Northern Germany, offering 4,600 square meters of office space on seven stories. The main investor and tenant is an organic supermarket chain that appreciates green ambitions.

The building's surroundings are very heterogeneous and consist of old warehouses and new solitary structures on the waterfront. Together with its western neighbor, H7 forms a forecourt where both main entrances are located. H7 stands on an elongated, north-south-oriented property and has a stepped cubature that follows the requirements for the distance between buildings. This has the advantage that the offices of the main tenant and all other twelve rental units each have their own terrace. Below the building is a semi-recessed parking garage. Its parking deck is framed so that it can be integrated into the building volume.

The main entrance on the western longitudinal façade leads into a partially two-story lobby. On the ground floor there is also a seminar area and a bistro, as well as showers and changing rooms for cyclists. On top of this are freely dividable office floors with a double-rowed, reinforced concrete central axis as the backbone, where all the ancillary rooms and the circulation areas are found. Like the service core, the basement and the ground floor of the building are made of reinforced concrete. Above it is a reinforced concrete structure with wood concrete composite slabs.

"The imperfect and non-plannable quality of a ceramic cladding as an alternative draft to the styled and cool façade of many new buildings"

While the head sides of the building are completely glazed and offer a view into its wooden interior, the side walls are clad with 3.5-centimeter-thick, glazed ceramic tiles in three different variants of a rich moss green. They are arranged in color patches, each comprising a parapet field and a pillar, and distributed in such a way that the same color tones never collide. The individual plates are 1.35 meters wide and either 50 or 40 centimeters high. Using specially designed nosepieces, they received a finely structured, horizontal relief with a groove spacing of 25 to 100 millimeters. This relief overlays the horizontal plate joints, gives the façade a depth effect, and makes it look like a moss-green checkered cloth laying over the building. [ab]

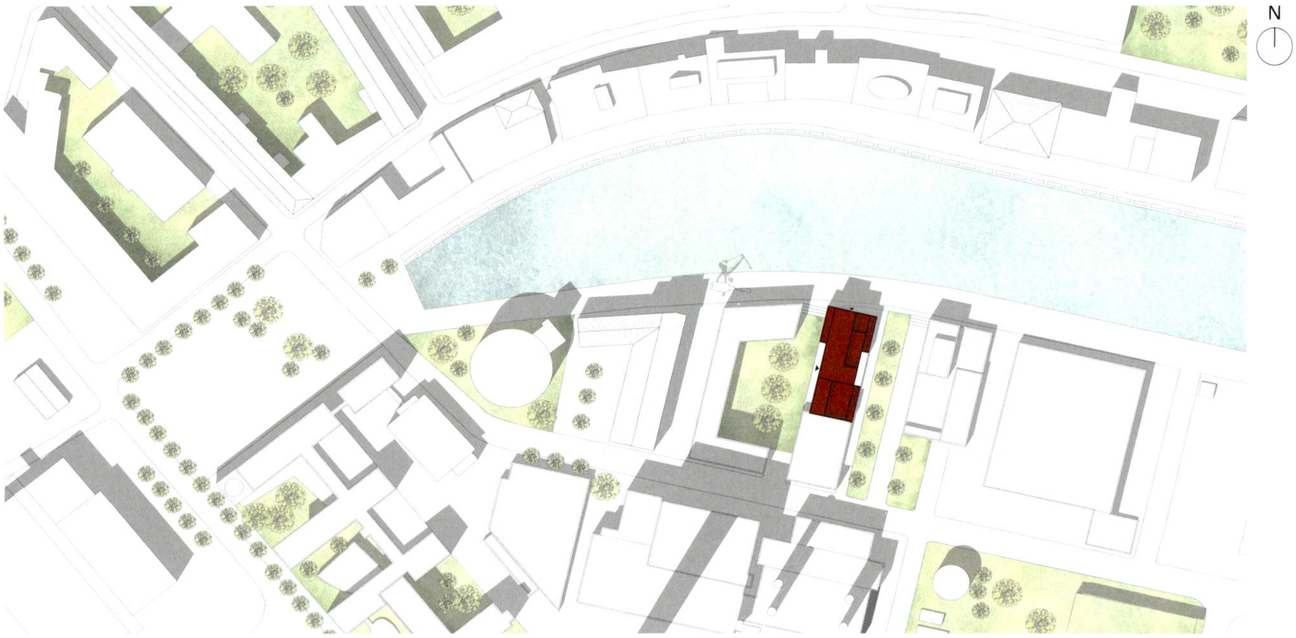

Site plan

Panels made of glazed, textured ceramic elements lend the façade a high-quality and finely stepped effect.

ARCHITEKTENKOMBINATIE BOS HOFMAN

Grofsmederij Rotterdam

Dennis Hofman and Fred Bos

PROJECT NAME
Grofsmederij Rotterdam

ARCHITECT/S
Architektenkombinatie Bos Hofman, Den Haag/ The Netherlands

BUILDING PURPOSE
Offices, education, culture, business

LOCATION
Rotterdam, The Netherlands

CONSTRUCTION PERIOD
2016–2017

BRICK TYPE
Facing bricks

BRICK AWARD CATEGORY
Working together

At one time, the RDM shipyard was one of the most important shipbuilding and repair facilities in the Netherlands. The Rotterdamsche Droogdok Maatschappij (Rotterdam Dry Dock Company) started operations in 1904 on the south bank of the Maas River and not only produced ocean-going vessels, but also submarines. After bankruptcy in 1983, the shipyard remained vacant for decades.
A rediscovery of the complex has only recently taken place: It now houses, among others, the Rotterdam Academy of Architecture and Urban Design, several departments of the Rotterdam University of Applied Sciences, a makerspace and a summer branch of the Museum Boijmans van Beuningen.
A water bus line connects the area with the city center.

Although it occupies a particularly prominent vantage point at the eastern end of the shipyard, right on the Maas, the blacksmith forge and boiler factory complex was still in miserable condition. Built in expressionist style by Jan Baanders in 1920, the boiler factory consists of a steel structure with shed roofs, surrounded by free-standing clinker brick walls. Above the orthogonal plinth, the fairly closed façades feature a folding motif that not only serves a structural function, but also lends the building monumentality. In 1938, the north wall of the boiler factory was removed and the industrial-looking blacksmith forge designed by architect Antonius Stoopman was added. Its clinker façades are broken up by vertical window strips with steel frames. On the head side is a 7 × 18-meter-large lifting gate.

"Redeveloping the industrial brickwork warehouses in the former RDM shipyard created an ecosystem for students and entrepreneurs in Rotterdam."

Presenting itself as a single, large space, the machine hall was carefully restored and now accommodates several commercial users. Later installations were removed, the concealed shed roofs opened, bricked up lifting gates uncovered and equipped with new doors.
A new, generously glazed main entrance offers an insight into the steel construction of the hall from the outside. Inside, the space compartments were aligned parallel to the old crane tracks so that the structure was preserved.

Due to rusting mounting anchors, the boiler factory façades had partly collapsed and were reconstructed as a three-layer cavity wall. Both buildings have restored original roof edges, rowlocks and ornaments. New, handmolded bricks with the original texture and color were made for this purpose: 122,000 bricks for the boiler factory and 144,000 bricks for the blacksmith forge. To make the patchwork even more inconspicuous, new parts of the façade were matched to the patina of the old brick buildings with spray paint. Once again the blacksmith forge and boiler factory act as figureheads of the RDM shipyard. [ab]

The building complex was restored inside and outside, partly freed of fixtures and partially reonstructed.

GROFSMEDERIJ
KETELMAKERIJ

SCHEIDT KASPRUSCH ARCHITEKTEN AND BBP : ARCHITEKTEN BDA

New Depot Building Hesterberg Schleswig-Holstein State Museum

Hermann Scheidt

PROJECT NAME
New Depot Building Hesterberg Schleswig-Holstein State Museum

ARCHITECT/S
Scheidt Kasprusch Architekten, Berlin/Germany, and bbp : architekten BDA, Kiel/Germany

BUILDING PURPOSE
Depot building

LOCATION
Schleswig, Germany

CONSTRUCTION PERIOD
2016–2018

BRICK TYPE
Hand-shaped bricks with troughs

BRICK AWARD CATEGORY
Working together

For decades, the Schleswig-Holstein Provincial Museums Foundation has been looking for a home for the extensive archives of the seven state museums in its care. Collectively, the museums tell the story of Schleswig-Holstein and the history of its people from the Stone Age to the present day. Its collections focus on archaeology, art, ethnology and cultural history, and with a million finds from archaeological excavations alone, the archive problem has been serious.

The solution was to restore and use former barracks, warehouses, a former grain store and a historic military magazine at Hesterberg, now a suburb of Schleswig and close to the Foundation's headquarters at Schloss Gottorf, a Baroque palace with medieval roots. The plan included a new and extendable building. This is the two-story museum depot designed by Scheidt Kasprusch architects of Berlin with the Kiel-based studio bbp : architekten.

The new storage depot, realized in a wholly contemporary style, completes an ensemble of museum buildings. Its flat, precise façade features panels of light gray brick without expansion joints alternating with dark steel-framed windows, doors and ventilation flaps. The aim here has been to shape a building that is finely crafted in a distinctly modern way and uses a refined if cool color scheme that plays against the more overtly colored brickwork and architectural details of the historic buildings. The concrete interior of the storage building is wholly functional, offering sophisticated and mostly natural cooling and ventilation.

What is important here is that the storage depot has been considered as a part of a coherent development of historic buildings. It is not a ready-made warehouse positioned casually for its purpose, but a bespoke design that also lives up to its function as a custodian of valued artifacts.

"The aim here has been to shape a building that is finely crafted in a distinctly modern way."

As such, it is a building that belongs to a long and noble tradition of storage buildings ranging through history from stately medieval tithe barns to ingeniously engineered aircraft hangars and Buckminster Fuller's geodesic domes. When we store things that are precious to us, it seems right that storage buildings themselves should be considered designs, well-made and even a delight to the eye. Too often they are treated as after-thoughts suggesting we value neither them nor their contents.

Architecturally, this new museum depot is a continuation of the work of the Scheidt Kasprusch studio that, significantly, includes an extension of the Staatliches Museum Schwerin realized in what the architects describe as "clear geometry and modest reduction" that works in harmony with existing historic buildings. To succeed in such contexts, this reductive approach to design demands precision and an ability to use materials whether timber, steel, glass or brick with intelligence and conviction. These qualities are evident in the design of the Museumsdepot Hesterberg. [jg]

If needed, the new building can be expanded.

Reduction and precision are the means of design.

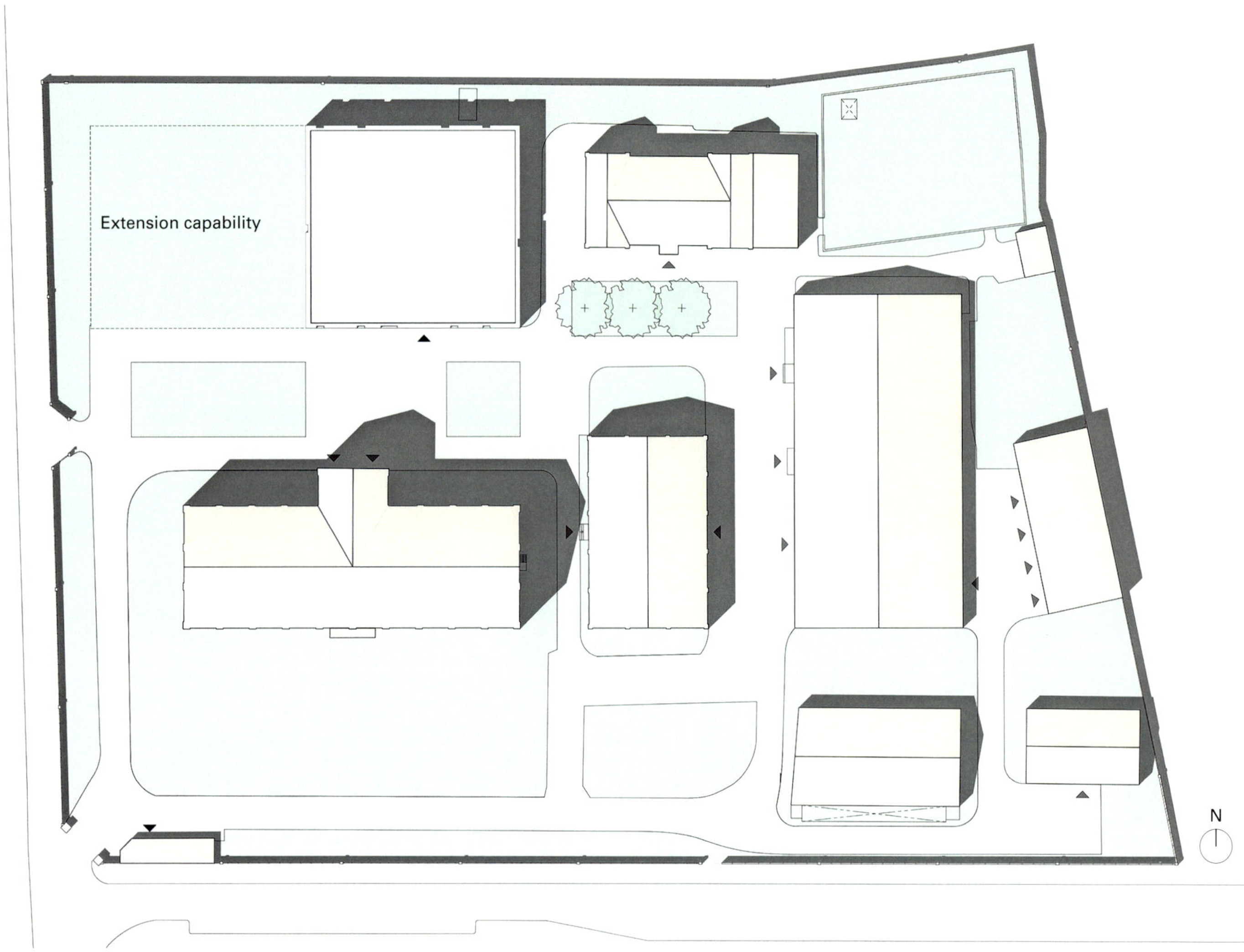

Site plan

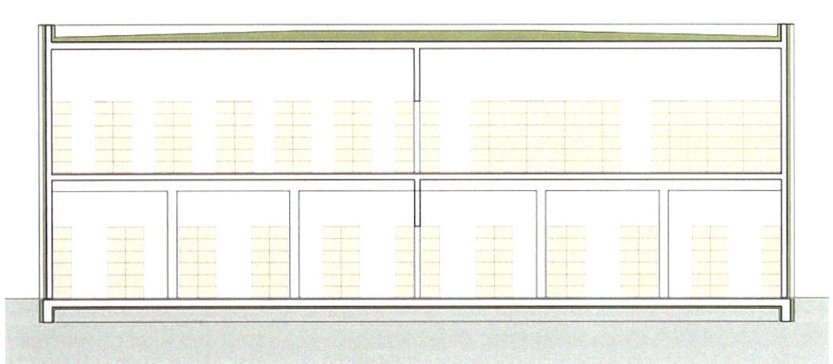

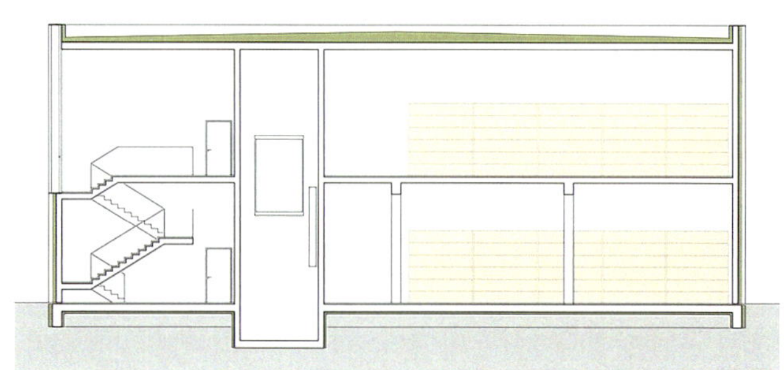

Sections

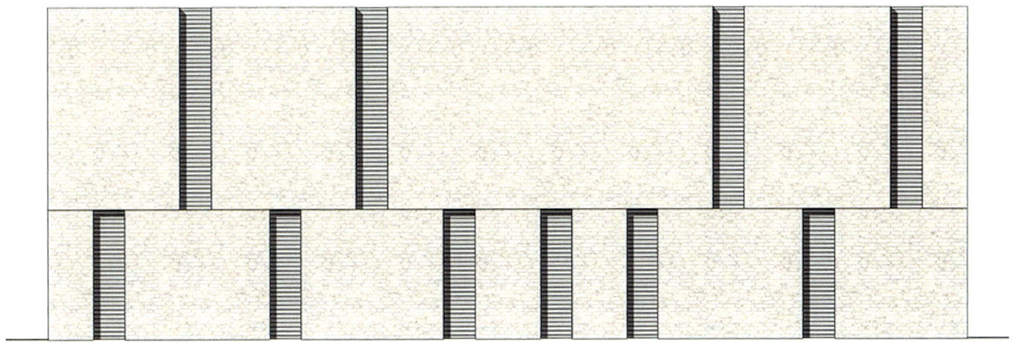
Elevation from the north

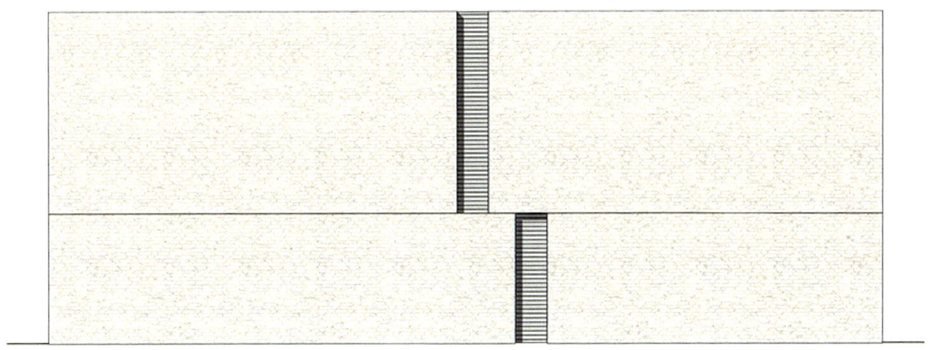
Elevation from the east

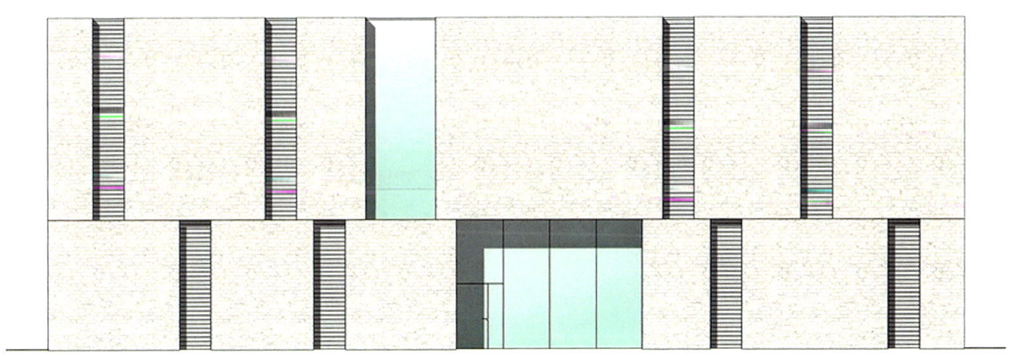
Elevation from the south

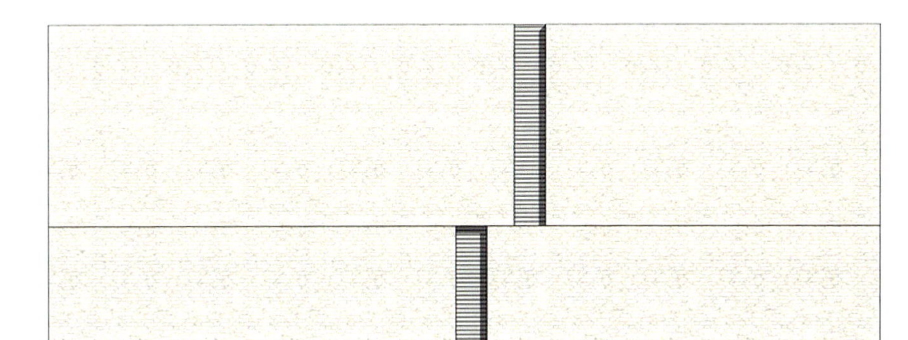
Elevation from the west

BETINA HANEL & MANFRED SANDNER

Tourism Information Center Innsbruck

Betina Hanel and Manfred Sandner

PROJECT NAME
Tourism Information Center Innsbruck

ARCHITECT/S
Betina Hanel & Manfred Sandner, Innsbruck/Austria

BUILDING PURPOSE
Offices, tourism information center

LOCATION
Innsbruck, Austria

CONSTRUCTION PERIOD
2018–2019

BRICK TYPE
Ceramic façade panels

BRICK AWARD CATEGORY
Working together

These subtle, but elaborately ornamented window coverings do not to attract attention at first glance. You have to look carefully to see them—but they are not supposed to be boastful. They blend into the former Innsbruck city wall and preserve the closed, unified effect it had maintained until the early 20th century. The artful play of ornamentation first becomes clearly visible at night, when the ornate arabesque grids made of clay tiles are backlit from the inside.

> "Each tile is evidently unique… a combination of archaic handicraft and modern design… a contemporary closing of the wounds in the 800-year-old city wall."

Originating from 1580, the Hofstall once housed horse stables on the ground floor and integrates parts of the old city wall. Used at various times for military purposes, the city acquired the building in 1921 and broke large windows through on the ground floor to better illuminate the three-aisled hall and its historical vaulting located behind. Today, it is the home of the municipal tourist information center, which was renovated in 2018. For this purpose, fixtures from the 1990s were removed, the floor lowered to its original level, the vault exposed and complemented where necessary. Diagonally opposite the existing main entrance, the architects created an additional entrance, so that the direction of spatial perception is shaped by an exciting diagonal perspective.

Made of Höttinger breccia, a conglomerate-like natural stone consisting of angular-shaped rock debris in a fine-grained matrix, the columns and the massive walls were refurbished. The exterior walls on the room side were toned down by a white paint; on the outside, their rough and porous character stands out in an undisguised manner.

Added in 1921, the arch-shaped windows held little regard for the vaults and façades. The special task faced by the architects was to eliminate this disruption without closing the openings as if nothing had happened.

In consultation with the Federal Monuments Office, a solution that works with a new component, namely tiles, yet honors the original building stock, was found.

Fired in a Japanese technique at low temperature and consisting of two differently colored clays, the tiles were made in a Vorarlberg manufactory. The pattern was developed using digital graphics. Here, the basic motif was superimposed in two layers and the upper shifted against the lower and rotated by 45 degrees. The combination of clay and loam, mixed with quartz sand and fireclay, the burning in a short time at 1,000 degrees Celsius and handcrafting provide space for happenstance: Gray earthy, porous tiles with a haptic structure arise, harmonizing ideally with the existing façade into which they were accurately inserted in a metal frame. Each tile is unique; the result is a cladding with a very special and extraordinary effect. [ch]

The arch on the interior is overlaid by the rectangular brick lattice on the outer wall.

The delicate structure of the tile pattern stands in contrast to the vaulted ceilings and the massive columns.

The depth of the structure arises from the two layers of brick tile twisted towards each other.

TCHOBAN VOSS ARCHITEKTEN

Commercial Building Große Bleichen

Ekkehard Voss

PROJECT NAME
Commercial Building Große Bleichen

ARCHITECT/S
TCHOBAN VOSS Architekten, Hamburg/Germany

BUILDING PURPOSE
Offices, retail

LOCATION
Hamburg, Germany

CONSTRUCTION PERIOD
2015–2018

BRICK TYPE
Facing bricks

BRICK AWARD CATEGORY
Working together

In the city center of Hamburg, an elongated, narrow, vacant lot was squeezed between the heritage-protected Alte Post (Old Post Office), built in 1847, and the recently listed, postmodern Galleria building from 1983. 80 meters long and only 14 meters wide, the property stretched from Große Bleichen street to the Bleichenfleet canal on the southeast side of the block. Tchoban Voss Architekten filled the gap with an office and commercial building that cleverly communicates between its historic and its historicizing neighbor, but at the same time has an unmistakably modern, overall form.

"The new office and commercial building closes a gap in the midst of historic brick buildings."

Retail spaces connecting the street to the fleet are located on the ground floor and first floor of the office and commercial building. Small-scaled and contiguously rentable office spaces, structured and illuminated by four light wells, occupy the four floors above.

The different eaves heights of the neighboring buildings are continued in angled sections in the two identical façades. A sculptural, backdrop-like staggering with several recesses arises, enabling the new structure to fit seamlessly into its context. Various-sized, floor-to-ceiling windows with anodized aluminum frames define the façade design. Nearly invisible glass balustrades were placed in front of the French windows on the upper floors. Slightly recessed frames in the masonry around the windows accentuate the gradation of the composition and lend it spatial depth.

"For the architectural bridging between old and new, clinker was chosen as façade material. In combination with contemporary formal language, the material harmoniously blends into the existing building structure."

Common in Hamburg, a dark red clinker was used for the façades,—but in this case it comes from Denmark. It is a waterstruck, coal-fired brick in the Danish standard dimension, laid in a freestyle bond. Firing the bricks with coal creates a lively play of light and dark color nuances and no two bricks are the same.

From a distance, the building appears a bit darker than its neighbors. When viewed from close up, however, it contains bricks that tie in with the color scheme of Alte Post and Galleria, and thus close the circle. [ab]

GALLERIA
GALLERIA
ALTE POST
PONTON

The horizontal structure of the new building reflects that of the neighbor building.

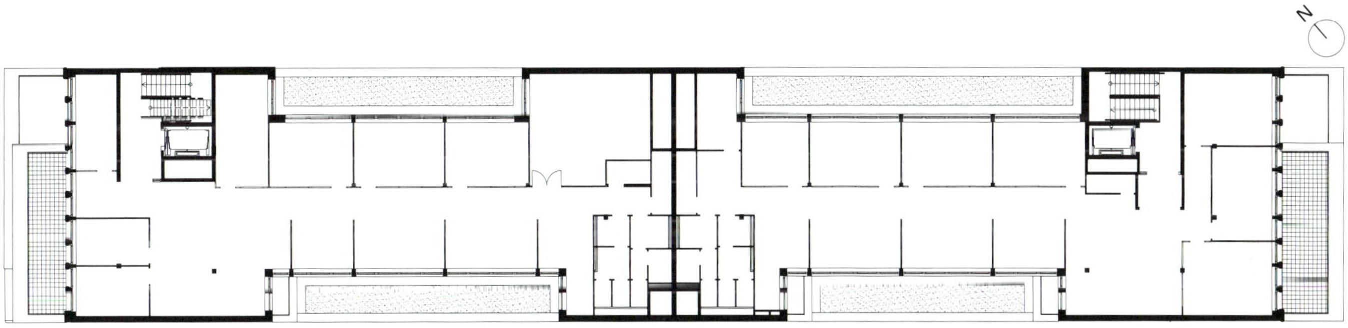

Fifth floor

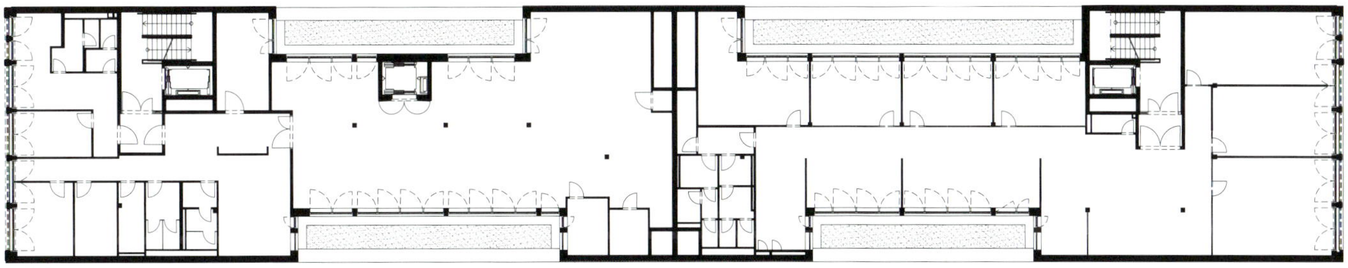

Second floor

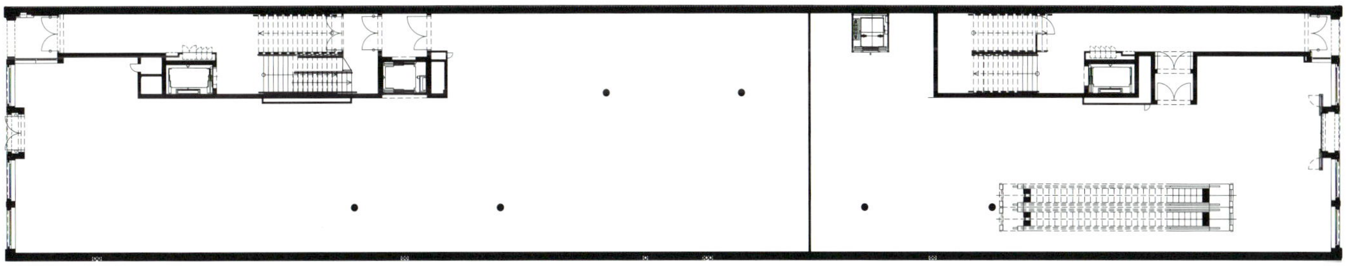

Ground floor

CASPER MUELLER KNEER ARCHITECTS

Céline Cheongdam

Jens Casper, Marianne Mueller and Olaf Kneer

PROJECT NAME
Céline Cheongdam

ARCHITECT/S
Casper Mueller Kneer Architects, London/GB

BUILDING PURPOSE
Offices, retail

LOCATION
Seoul, Korea

CONSTRUCTION PERIOD
2016–2017

BRICK TYPE
Facing bricks

BRICK AWARD CATEGORY
Working together

Céline Vipiana and her husband, Richard, founded Céline, the Parisian fashion house, in 1945. It began life as a made-to-measure children's shoe shop famous for its red elephant logo created by the cartoonist Raymond Peynet on rue de Malte in the 11th arrondissement. Soon enough, Vipiana launched her own prêt-à-porter clothing range for women. The number of Céline shops grew. Since 1996, Céline has been a part of the LVMH Group and today there are 150 Céline stores around the world.

This freestanding flagship seven-story building is located on a prominent site in Seoul's Cheongdam fashion quarter in the Gangnam District. Comprising shop and offices, it steps up and back from street level and is wrapped in a bespoke white- and gray-colored Italian brick cladding. The architects have chosen a complex bond using different lengths and openings to give the impression of a part opaque, part transparent fabric stretched tightly around the taut form of the building.

Flush mortar joints of matching color and exaggerated depth are introduced to enhance the monolithic quality of the façade. This brick skin is offset from the building's thermal envelope by a gap: a type of filter or semi-transparent shield.

To achieve a varied visual effect, the brick bond was designed on a computer, although the bricks themselves have been hand-laid by local bricklayers to achieve a crafted quality. By night, the full effect of this perforated architectural dress is revealed as the building is lit from within.

Casper Mueller Kneer have demonstrated how a brick building can exude a strong and even monumental presence while suggesting the tactile and intricate nature of clothing fabric.

> "Through this particular use of the material, the façade has a crafted, hand-made quality with a strong materiality and unique articulation."

In Seoul, where streets are often composed of rows of individual buildings, each on its own tight plot and with nothing in common in terms of architectural style, new developments — especially shops with something special to promote — are under pressure to be distinctive. Every new building cries for attention. The Céline store is an attempt to be noticed while not shouting. In terms of Gangnam style, it offers presence and manners. [jg]

CÉLINE
CÉLINE

The brick bond was digitally designed and hand-laid.

During the day the building seems monolithic; at night the light radiates out from the inside.

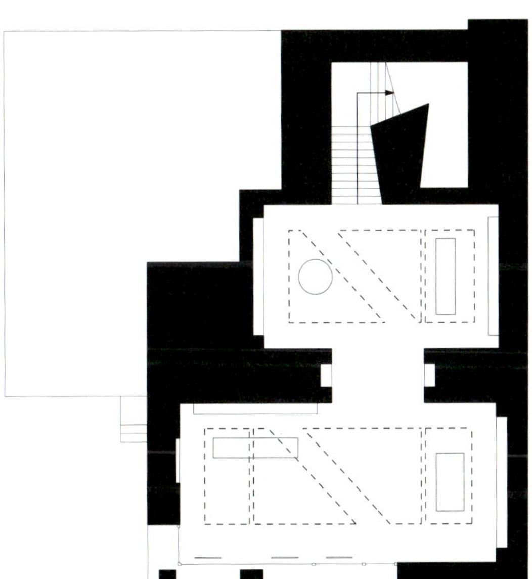
Ground floor

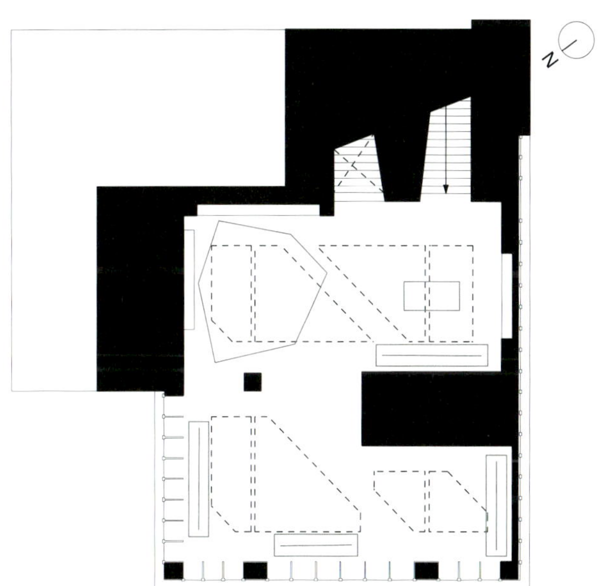
First floor

Sharing public spaces

AGLAÉE DEGROS

Transformation of the Public Space

Aglaée Degros

Urban Public Space

The pressures on public spaces in city centers are both from *museification* and *evenementization,* to which the *securitization* has been added in recent years. "If every space is susceptible to attack and every person a potential attacker, then the only recourse is to watch everyone and fortify every place," Mr. Sorkin teaches us.[1] We can conclude that public space is currently subject to so many different interests that in a large number of city centers its control and regulation become obstacles to its character.

In such a context, it can be observed that public buildings often are conceived as a space participating in the public domain, a shelter placed in a continuous public space. An example is the Juridicum in Vienna, where two of my students established their office in the entrance hall for a day. By this they highlighted that it is much easier to organize your office in a university building than on a public bench from where you are dislodged much more quickly by the police. It can be concluded that there are places in urban centers that have become more public than public space.[2]

Some buildings in this book have similarities with this example, treating the inside-outside relationship with the same spirit of coherence, such as the kult center. Thanks to its fully glazed ground floor and the continuity of the exterior and interior ground levels, the façade on the ground floor looks more like a need for thermal separation than a barrier. The same applies to the fluidity of the ground floor in the case of Teglen Spikkestad, which is undoubtedly an excellent example of the desire that the building should be an integral part of the public space: a glazed façade with a light exterior structure and a continuity of the ground surface. Obviously, the integration of public buildings depends not only on their formalization or materialization, but also on their administration. The functions and management of the latter is a decisive factor in its public nature: many public places could be inspired by more open and tolerant management. The library of the city of Heidenheim deals with this topic by combining architecture and function tending towards public appropriation. On the one hand, the fluidity between exterior and interior space is realized thanks to the absence of a plinth and the continuity of the exterior surface without any difference in level; on the other hand, by its programming and by integrating an intergenerational café.

Parochial Space

The transformations of public space mentioned above are not uniformly imposed throughout the urban territory and some areas are more sensitive to commercialization, security and Disneyfication than others. These trends are, for example, much less prevalent in residential districts that do not meet the requirements of city marketing. In these more remote districts, a transformation of public space into parochial space often happens with the support of civil society actors. It is the sociologist Lyn Lofland who distinguished the parochial space from public spaces. She characterized it as a public space appropriated by a certain group of the population. Since public spaces are a reflection of the society that created them, they have taken on various forms and names through time and across civilizations. It is clear that outside urban centers the culture of the self often prevails over otherness.[3] We are witnessing more and more different interests between residents, commuters, tourists and commercial actors. This constitutes a movement where inhabitants reclaim the public space: the transformation of the park into a vegetable garden, a playground with controlled access, etc. Panerai and Castex, in their book on the urban form,[4] refer to the "close," developed in the garden cities, which is a space, often a series of lawns, surrounded by houses with small gardens slightly separated from the main street, a little bit like a "cul-de-sac." It is a public space where no one who does not live nearby would dare to organize a picnic!

In such a context, architects create structural units that consist of a public building and a section that sets itself apart from real public space through its shape, materialization or arrangement in the overall context. One could even consider the kindergarten in the village of Xinchang as a true implementation of the "close," whereby the section here is not a lawn, but a paved courtyard. The brick façades of the surrounding buildings form an entity that stands out clearly from the surroundings. This idea is taken one step further in the Sanhe Village Center project by marking the outside spaces with walls and thus becoming an integral part of the building.

> "If the public space is to be truly shared, it must give way to otherness."

Otherness[5]

Even if parochial spaces are justified in certain contexts, the "real" public space is characterized by the possibility of shared use. It has to allow "otherness" so that the most diverse population groups can move in it and encounter one another. Jacques Lévy explains in his book on spatial justice that *altérité* can only develop in an open environment where meeting the other is possible. Isn't public space by definition a place of social encounter? "A place where various pathways intersect, where various trajectories merge and are sometimes confronted with the other. There are places where culture meets politics, where social territories merge with individual territories."[6] The search for fluidity between the building and the public space certainly goes in this direction, but also the search for the opening of parochial spaces. In this sense, the Storey's Field Centre and Eddington Nursery project tries to integrate into the urban structure; it seems to be a part of the environment. Nevertheless, the garden does not participate in this open approach ... In the years to come, should we not question this approach to parochial space? Like we, in recent years, have questioned the museification, marketing and security of the city centers? After all, Waldkindergartens have no limits, there are high schools integrated into the urban texture without any grid or barrier. Isn't that our role as designers to create a framework conducive to otherness... a nice work *in situ* for future generations of students...?

1 Michael Sorkin, *Indefensible Space,* London: Routledge, 2007.
2 Bastian Vollert, Tobias Richter, *Unmöglich oeffentlich?* IKA/ Acadamy of Fine Arts Vienna, Master thesis, Vienna: 2014.
3 Lyn Lofland, *The Public Realm,* Hawthorne, NY: Aldine de Gruyter, 1999.
4 Jean Castex, Jean-Charles Depaule, Philippe Panerai, *Formes urbaines: de l îlot à la barre,* Marseille: Éditions Parenthèses, 1977.
5 Jacques Lévy, Jean-Nicolas Fauchille, Ana Póvoas, *Théorie de la justice spatiale,* Paris: Éditions Odile Jacob, 2018.
6 Ali Madanipour, *Public and Private Space of the City,* London: Routledge, 2003.

BAAS ARQUITECTURA WITH GRUPA 5 ARTCHITEKCI AND MAŁECCY BIURO PROJEKTOWE

Silesia University's Radio and TV Department in Katowice

Jordi Badia, Mikołaj Kadłubowski,

Krzysztof Mycielski, Rafał Zelent and Wojciech Małecki

PROJECT NAME
Silesia University's Radio and TV Department in Katowice

ARCHITECT/S
BAAS Arquitectura (Barcelona/Spain) with Grupa 5 artchitekci (Warsaw/Poland) and Małeccy biuro projektowe (Katowice/Poland)

BUILDING PURPOSE
Education

LOCATION
Katowice, Poland

CONSTRUCTION PERIOD
2014–2017

BRICK TYPE
Facing bricks

BRICK AWARD CATEGORY
Sharing public spaces

BRICK 20 Grand Prize Winner

Historically and architecturally, Katowice is a richly layered if darkly cinematic city. In the 19th century, its coalmines, steel mills, foundries and brickworks paid for grand boulevards, imposing monuments and rows of muscular, working class tenement housing. Fought over by the Nazis and Soviets in the 1940s, it was ravaged and then partly rebuilt with soulless high-rise apartment blocks as old city streets and their battered though handsome buildings were torn down.

Today, this southern Polish city is known for its culture rather than coal mining. Here, though, on Pawła Street in the Chiaroscuro core of the city, is a magical new building that marries Katowice's history to the city's future. A surviving dark brick tenement building—once home to Silesian coal miners—has been renovated and wrapped in a screen or net curtain of bricks sheltering a new university faculty of radio and television occupying a large courtyard complex.

The effect from the cobbled street lined with frayed 19th century buildings is powerful. This is architecture as "film noir." Behind the dark brick screen, the faculty building opens up into new spaces, light when they need to be, shadowy and even a little dark, too, with classrooms and studios surrounding the inner courtyard. Brickwork throughout is varied, thoughtful and well-crafted.

> "The dark and stained brick is full of meanings that speak about the past and the Silesian coal mines."

The brick curtain is made of the same material as the surviving 19th century house, so the building has a consistency of texture. This perforated screen, however, is as light as the house is dark, even though this is not immediately apparent when the building is first seen from the street. In fact, it brings patterns and nuances of daylight into the heart of this courtyard building, playing on surfaces—walls, floors, ceilings, stairs—faced in subtly changing shades of the same brick.

These bricks—burned for longer or shorter periods in one of Europe's last coal-fuelled kilns—are nuanced with dark sintering and graduations of color and used throughout the building. The rich ceramic texture penetrates deeply into the university's interior, creating a singular atmosphere enhanced by daylight playing through the screen facing Pawła Street. In itself, the building is a master class in subtle lighting techniques.

The architects—from Barcelona, Warsaw and Katowice—say their aim was "not to create an iconic structure, but to complement a particular fragment of the city." They wanted "to analyze what already existed, discover why it was so special and then lend it a unique atmosphere and personality. In this case new architecture was supposed to become a background that would naturally add a finishing touch to the already existing urban space."

Even so, the architects have created a distinctive and memorable building that will undoubtedly attract visitors keen to see and experience it. It does, however, show how a city center building can be innovative and, at the same time, a guardian and interpreter of the past. This is a haunting design and a pitch perfect setting for film students. [jg]

Jury statement

"A radical, yet subtle approach seemingly elevates the existing historic fabric of a Katowice street imbued with Silesian coal history. A dark shaded, open brick lattice entirely wraps a modestly existing, multi-family coalminers' house, which also housed a light bulb production, into an abstract larger structure as opposed to demolishing it. The subtle integration of the new university facility into the existing context resonates on several levels: on an urban and architectural level, as well as excessively on the material level, where the dark chromatics and patina of the bricks of the neighboring buildings were carefully mastered within the production of several types of new bricks for this unique educational project. An impressive realization of a highly conceptual public competition-winning proposal with the agenda of reuse and accentuated contextual sensitivity was a collective effort of three European architecture practices to highlight the unique atmosphere of the immediate surroundings."

A lattice structure arches over the existing building and closes the street front.

Entrance zone

The single-flight staircase leads up to the top floor.

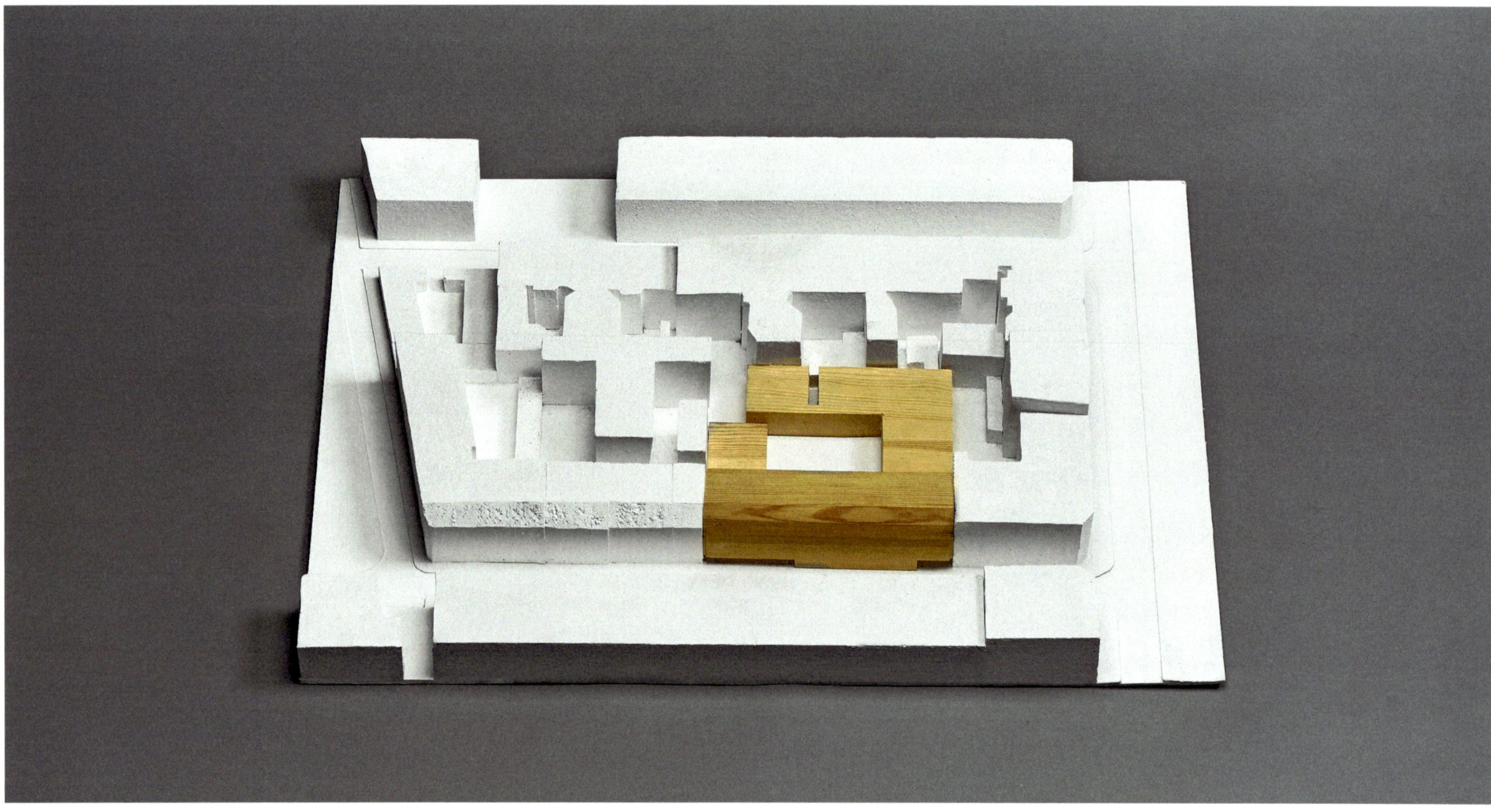

Structure model

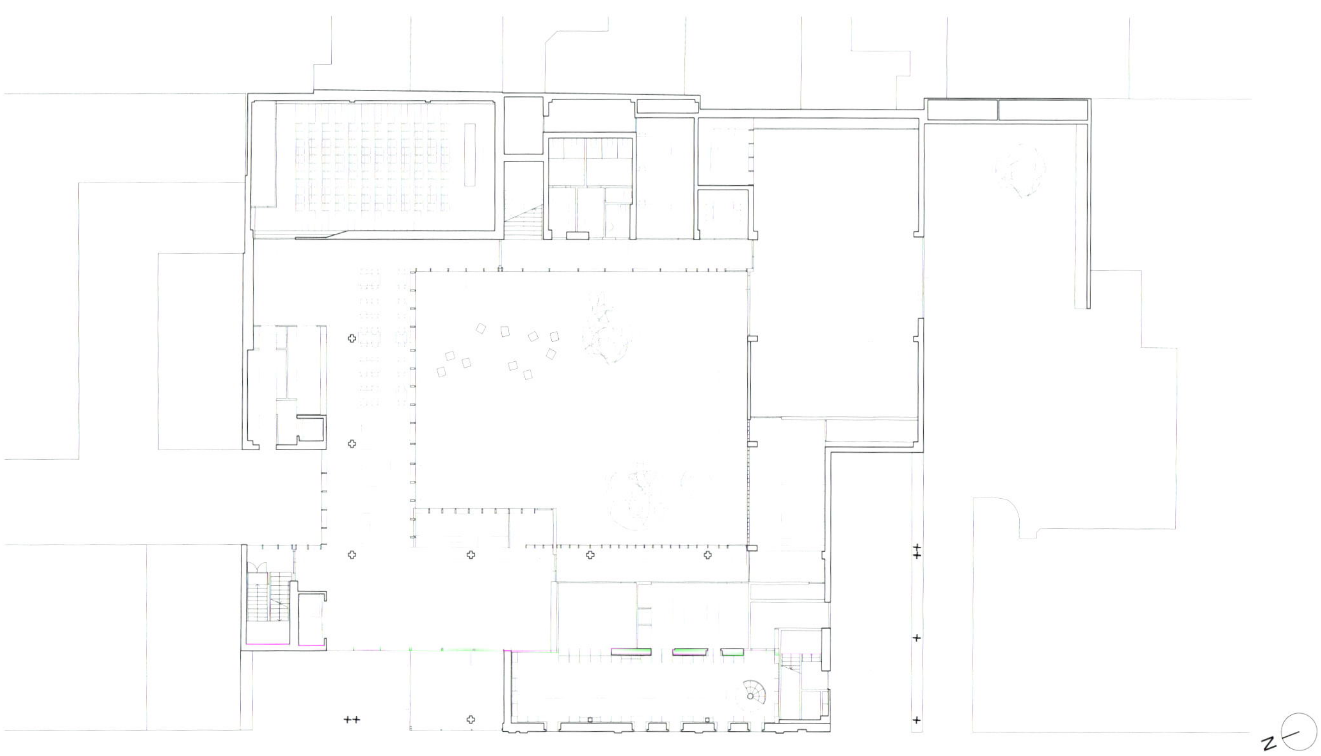

Ground Floor

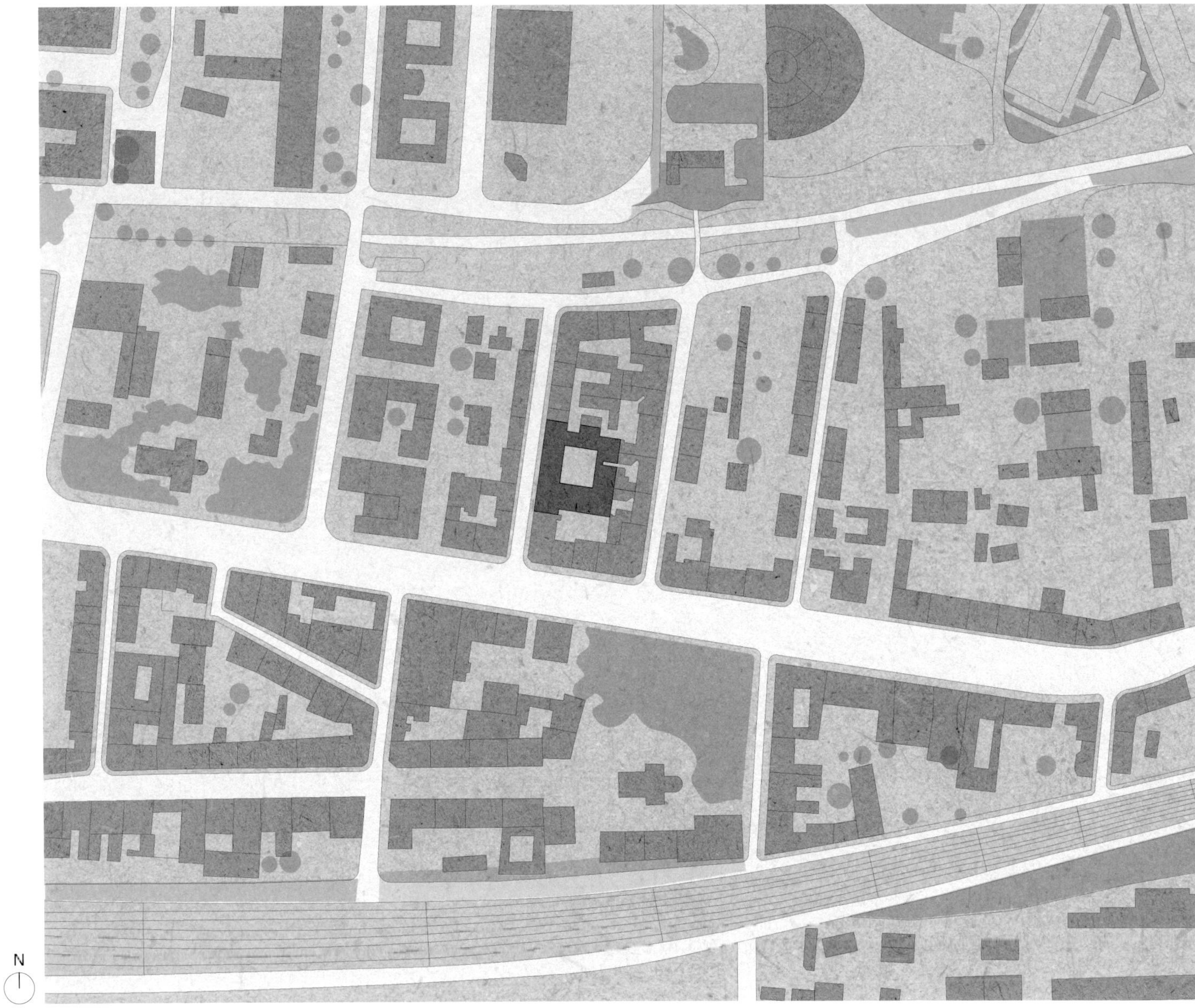

Site plan

Axonometry

Sharing public spaces

View from the courtyard side.

Sharing public spaces

Village Centre in Sanhe

Li Shaochong, Wang Maozhen and Wu Rui

PROJECT NAME
Village Centre in Sanhe

ARCHITECT/S
Xi'an University of Architecture and Technology (XAUAT) and Wall Architects Shaanxi/China

BUILDING PURPOSE
Housing, education, culture, leisure

LOCATION
Fuping/China

CONSTRUCTION PERIOD
2017–2018

BRICK TYPE
Facing bricks

BRICK AWARD CATEGORY
Sharing public spaces

BRICK 20 Honorary Mention

Situated in the central Chinese Guanzhong Plain, the village of Sanhe is typical for this region. Still strongly influenced by agriculture, it is nonetheless threatened by the loss of social and cultural cohesion. The new village center is an answer to this: It sees itself as a place where the more important material and immaterial heritage is concentrated — and becomes visible and tangible both in the architecture and in the usage. Moreover, the center serves to improve the provision of public social and economic infrastructure in rural areas.

"In contemporary Chinese rural architectural design, the most important element is to realize the self-adjustment ability of the buildings by the most concise, easy and straightforwardly feasible way."

The functions it is intended to unite comprise homes for the elderly, a rural health center, an information center, exhibition showrooms for rural industry and local history, a small library and reading rooms, a lecture space and prayer room, as well as recreational areas.

Since the requirement stipulated that craftsmen and building materials have to come from the region, the architects had to equally consider local and traditional construction methods and knowledge in order to achieve a convincing result.

The building stands on an elongated plot at the entrance to the village, in the second row behind a development with new apartment houses that runs along the access road. The architects opted for a predominantly single-story building, which receives a visual anchor in just one spot with a superstructure.

Strictly orthogonal, the structure is vividly varied by courtyards and the alternation of open and closed areas. Surrounded on all sides by brick walls, the full diversity of the village center first reveals itself inside. A central inner axis provides orientation; two passages connect the entrance side directly with the small grove bordering on the north. A forecourt, low walls, a ramp and steps mediate between the interior and exterior; a reddish-earthy-colored brick has been chosen not only for the brick walls, but also throughout the house as flooring, so that concentrated unity with respect to the variety of functions comes to the fore. The brick only stands back somewhat in the white-painted interiors.

The focus on the interior is further enhanced by the treatment of the openings: Walls laid in gaps were set in front of them as an open grid structure. Bricks cover all windows except those in the interior, towards the courtyards. The recessed entrance areas and passageways ensure that the house does not seem hermetic and unwelcoming.

Although the concrete skeleton structure on which the house is built remains visible, the dominant feature is the locally available red brick. Used in a core-insulated, double-shell construction, it incorporates the tradition and material-oriented directness of local building. [ch]

Honorary mention:
"The jury appreciated this project for its clear use of brick construction, which manages to suggest weight as well as fragility where the brickwork is stretched open. It is a clear and poetic response to a social program."

The sequence of paths and courtyards provides for permeability and lingering possibilities outdoors.

Scheme of paths, courtyards and closed areas

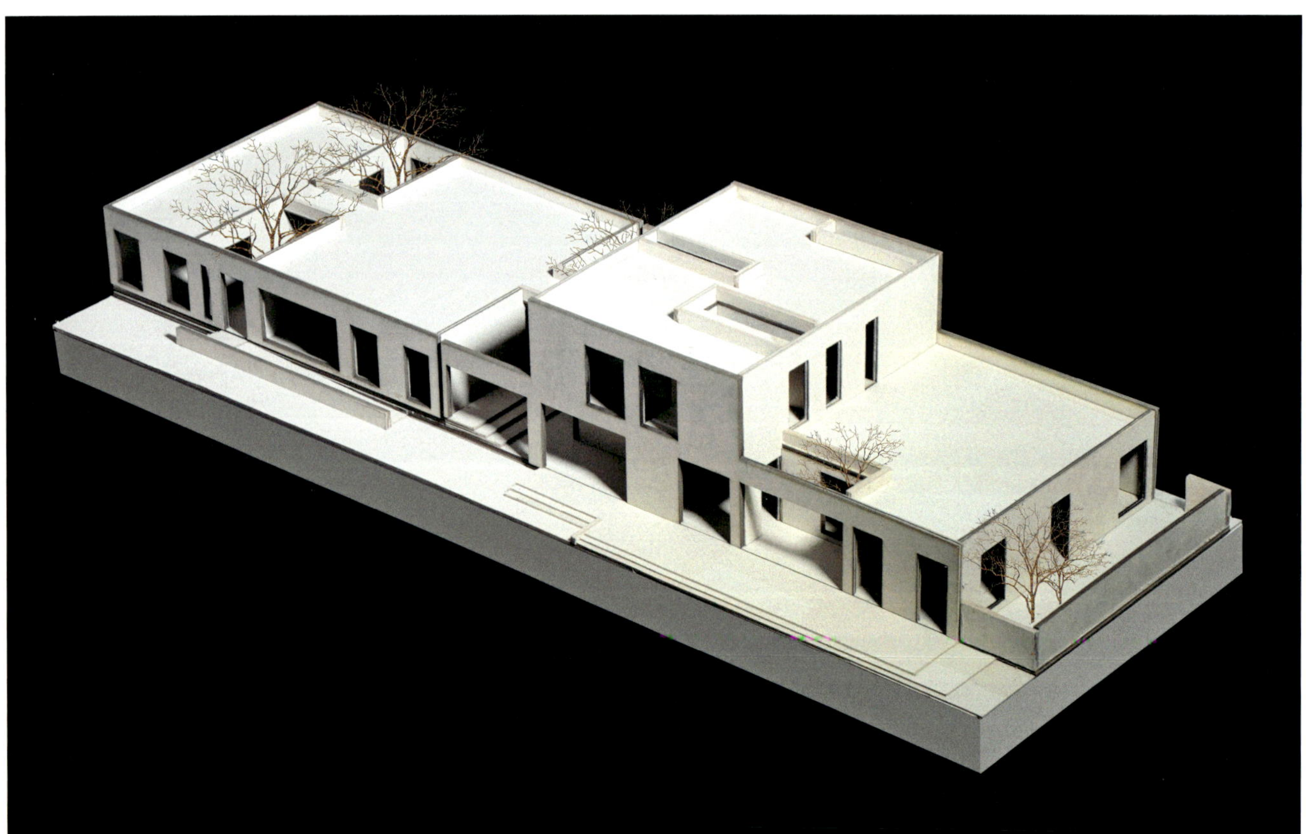

Model

Brick lattices were placed in front of the windows on the outer side of the complex.

Sharing public spaces

POOL LEBER ARCHITEKTEN

kult—Cultural Center Westmünsterland

Martin Pool and Isabella Leber

PROJECT NAME
kult—Cultural Center Westmünsterland

ARCHITECT/S
POOL LEBER ARCHITEKTEN, Munich/Germany

BUILDING PURPOSE
Culture

LOCATION
Vreden, Germany

CONSTRUCTION PERIOD
2013–2018

BRICK TYPE
Waterstruck coal-fired bricks

BRICK AWARD CATEGORY
Sharing public spaces

The historic city silhouette was the inspiration behind the design for the "kult," the new cultural-historical center of Vreden. At a central location, with the city library in the baroque palace and the parish and monastery churches in immediate proximity, the city near the Dutch border displays its gathered treasures. On the other side of the moat, the "cultural axis" continues up to a circular-shaped indoor sports arena and the former harbor area. As the main lynchpin of an urban concept that turns the rich history into a present-day cultural strength, "kult" combines a museum, an administrative office, an archive and a scientific institute.

Naturally, the house is not entirely new: It includes buildings from the 1970s and 1980s, as well as takes in the adjoining historic structures from the 14th and 16th centuries: the Poorhouse and the Powder Tower, which were freed from annexes erected in the 1980s. Both belong to the few remnants of historical fabric spared from destruction during the war. Looking from a courtyard, the Poorhouse can now also be inspected from the outside, thus becoming part of the exhibition. The Powder Tower recalls the city wall and shows the course of the old city moat. The structures of the 1970s and 80s were adapted to serve as administrative office and archive. Retrofitted energetically, they were integrated into the overall complex, which now appears as an entity of different epochs and construction methods and, in a broader sense, also incorporates the two prominent Vreden brick buildings: the baroque palace and the parish church.

The original idea to leave the façades of the 40- to 50-year-old buildings was abandoned. They were in need of renovation, so the quiet overall impression was given preference. In order to accomplish this, despite the irregular roofscape, overhangs were avoided and windows set deeply, making the complex almost seem like a brick sculpture. The coal-fired clinkers used for the building envelope were slightly graded in terms of color, so that shades and nuances reveal the individual time strata at a glance. Detailing, references and proportions provide further information to the time of origin of the components.

> "Bricks unify the different buildings while enhancing their singular identities."

Centrally accessed from the square and opened across the entire height of the building, the foyer is characterized by strongly structured exposed concrete, which the rough-sawn formwork lends a brick-adequate, haptic quality to. The exhibition concept was also based on the historical spatial division into the secular monastery and the worldly city: the profane section of the exhibition is housed on the first floor, the sacred one on the second. Of course, the open stairwell ensures that the two are well-connected—just like the new "kult," which defines the marketplace, became the connecting hinge that links the parts of the city's history. [ch]

Existing buildings from various epochs were integrated into "kult."

The building borders directly on the city moat.

View looking from the church square

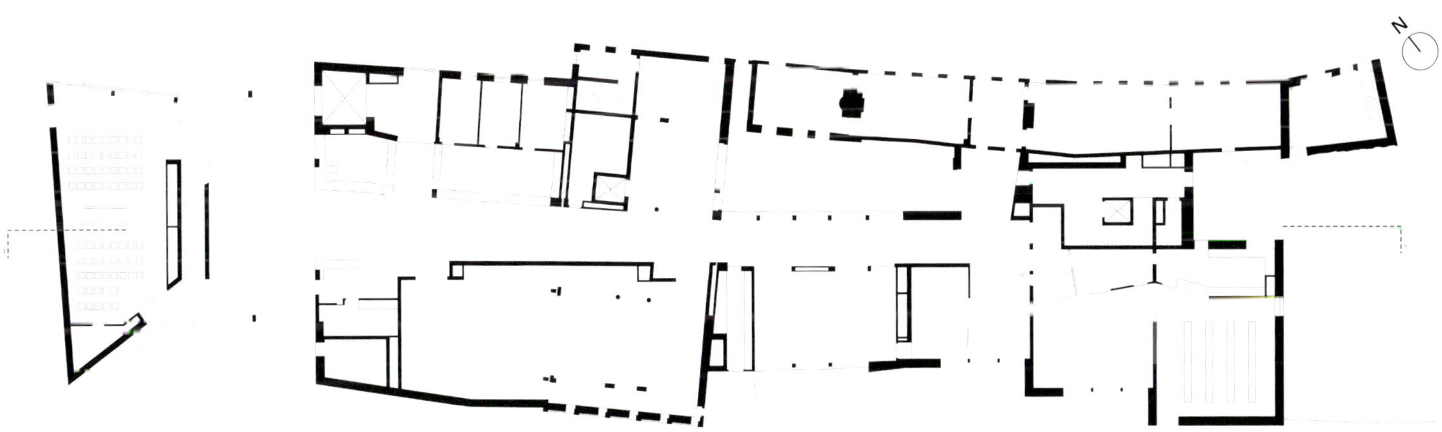

Ground floor

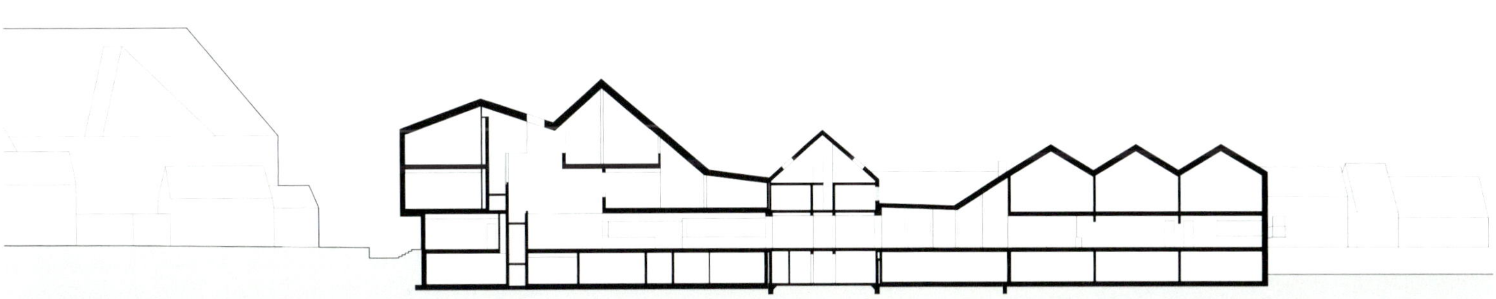

Longitudinal section

EINAR DAHLE ARCHITECTS MNAL AND HILLE MELBYE ARCHITECTS AS

"Teglen" Spikkestad Church and Culture Center

Mikkel Haavaldsen, Kaja Melbye, Joachim Midjo Andersen and Aina Dahle

PROJECT NAME
"Teglen" Spikkestad Church and Culture Center

ARCHITECT/S
Einar Dahle Architects MNAL and Hille Melbye Architects AS, Oslo/Norway

BUILDING PURPOSE
Sacred building, culture

LOCATION
Spikkestad, Røyken, Norway

CONSTRUCTION PERIOD
2016–2018

BRICK TYPE
Facing bricks, paving bricks

BRICK AWARD CATEGORY
Sharing public spaces

"Teglen," which means "The Brick" in Norwegian, might seem a blunt and irreverent name for a new parish church, and yet for the local community of Spikkestad, a village 40 kilometers southwest of Oslo, it is one of affinity and endearment. The new church and culture centre—the most impressive building in Spikkestad—is built on a site next door to a former brickworks. Today, a brick pavement that looks as if it has been rolled out like a carpet connects the church's commanding bell tower to the village railway station. The first thing visitors to the village see when they step down from trains at Spikkestad is this impressive new building, its façade studded with brick crosses.

Essentially, this is a concrete building faced in distinctive red brick. The powerful east façade, or bell tower, is designed to catch the eye of visitors to Spikkestad. It is also a reference to traditional Norwegian church towers and, in particular, a reference—that, presumably, only local people will make—to the towering brick chimneys of the former Spikkestad brick factory.

Although apparently massive in terms of construction, the building is filled with daylight, its ground floor wrapped with floor-to-ceiling glazing to create a seamless threshold between interior and exterior and, say the architects, to "maximize contact with the town square." At once a religious and a secular building, "The Brick" looks both outwards and inwards. The church itself can be enclosed as if cut off from the everyday world or connected to it when full-length, oak-veneered doors are folded aside to join sacred and ceremonial civic spaces. These are set above a café, offices and activity rooms.

> "A compact yet generous plan wrapped in brickwork for order and freedom"

The idea of a church and cultural or civic center sharing the same building and even the same interior spaces makes good sense in Norway, where until very recently the National or Evangelical Lutheran Church was synonymous with the state. Until 2017, clergy were civil servants performing civic roles that overlapped with those of religious practice. Today, although Norway professes to be perhaps the least "religious" European country, the Church and its buildings continue to play a key public role.

For Einar Dahle and Hille Melbye, the Teglen Spikkestad Church and Culture Centre is an "architecture that investigates the relationship between intimacy and distance, between the grandiose and the subtle and between the sacred and the secular". The difference in tone and atmosphere between the nominally divergent spaces inside is achieved through the subtlest change in the use of elemental materials—brick, timber and concrete—and, especially, through the manipulation of daylight. The church makes elegant use of top lighting, its interior bathed in diffused daylight. A place for communal services and quiet contemplation, this new church complex is a valuable social as well as spiritual hub for Spikkestad. [jg]

Sharing public spaces

The mighty east façade with the bell tower makes reference to the smokestacks of a former brickworks in the neigborhood.

Brick, wood and concrete are the dominating materials.

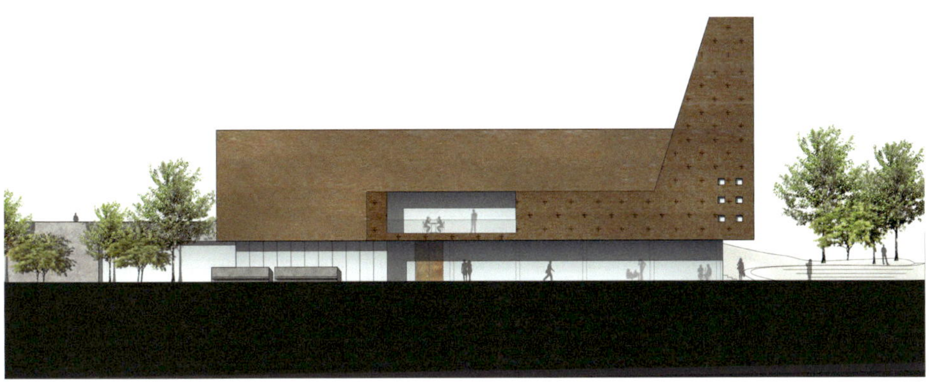

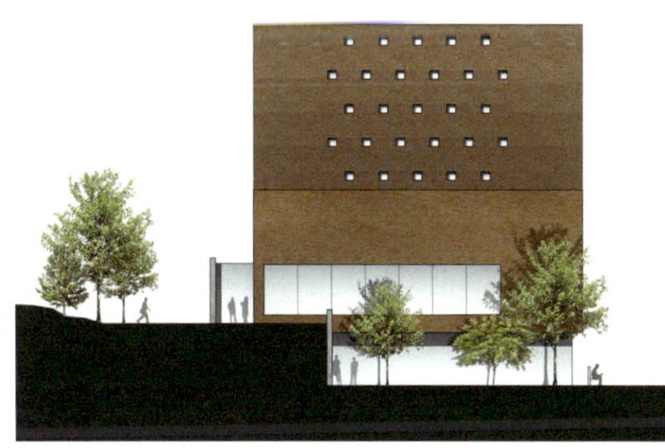

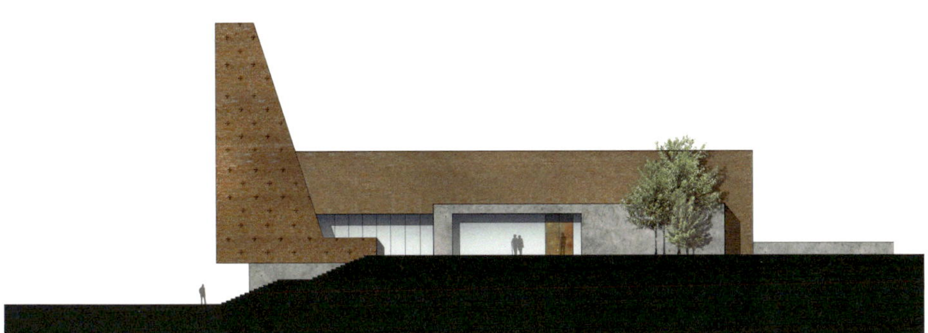

Elevations from the east, north, south and west clockwise from bottom right

ATELIER DESHAUS

Kindergarten of Xinchang Village

Chen Yifeng

PROJECT NAME
Kindergarten of Xinchang Village

ARCHITECT/S
Atelier Deshaus, Shanghai/China

BUILDING PURPOSE
Education

LOCATION
Yaan, China

CONSTRUCTION PERIOD
2016–2017

BRICK TYPE
Facing brick, paving brick

BRICK AWARD CATEGORY
Sharing public spaces

Xinchang is a riverside town sited at the junction of the Chengdu Plain and the Qionglai Mountains in Sichuan Province. The Tea and Horse Road passed this way in centuries gone by when Chinese tea was traded for Tibetan mules and Indian silks. Today, this is the route of the high-speed Sichuan-Tibet Railway, currently under construction and due to open in 2025.

Rapid development of the area was checked in April 2013 by the Lushan earthquake measuring 7.0 on the Richter scale. This new kindergarten set above Xinchang with carefully framed views of the mountain pass is one positive result of the devastating earthquake. It is one of ten new kindergartens in the region funded by the One Foundation, a non-governmental organization established in 2007 by Jet Li (Li Lianjie), the Chinese actor, film producer, martial artist and Chinese Red Cross ambassador.

The design of the Xinchang kindergarten is by the Shanghai studio Atelier Deshaus, founded in 2001 by Liu Yichun and Chen Yifeng. Instead of a single new building, the architects have designed the kindergarten in the guise of a stylized village. Nine "cottages" are clustered around a stepped, west-facing, U-shaped courtyard. Courtyard paving, steps, ramps and the façades of the individual buildings are made of locally sourced shale sintering bricks: the kindergarten is very much a part of the local landscape.

> "Bricks have brought the kindergarten a warm and homey atmosphere as we wished."

Shale brick is a common building material of local rural buildings admired for its excellent physical properties and appearance. Its use in the construction of the kindergarten is both respectful of local tradition and landscape and a way of creating a warm and homey feel inside and outside the building.

Because it rains heavily in Xinchang, brick passageways and a more or less continuous veranda link the buildings. Some of the passageways are painted red, a color associated in China with good fortune and happiness. Reveals of windows and walls in some of the "cottages" are yellow, a symbol of freedom from worldly concerns.

Very gently, the kindergarten children are encouraged to engage with the natural world. Walking outside and perhaps in the rain allows them to feel the elements and to see the mountainous landscape beyond both their "village" and Xinchang. The sound of rain pattering on the corrugated steel roofs of the veranda is also a reminder of the energy and joys of nature.

The Xinchang kindergarten demonstrates the inherent and enduring value of traditional Chinese courtyard housing. Today, whether in the design of schools, hotels, kindergartens and, of course, residential areas, it allows people to meet naturally, to walk in the open between classes or duties and, above all, to feel connected to the world outside the confines of hermetic, single purpose, modern buildings. [jg]

A kindergarten as a village

The inner courtyard

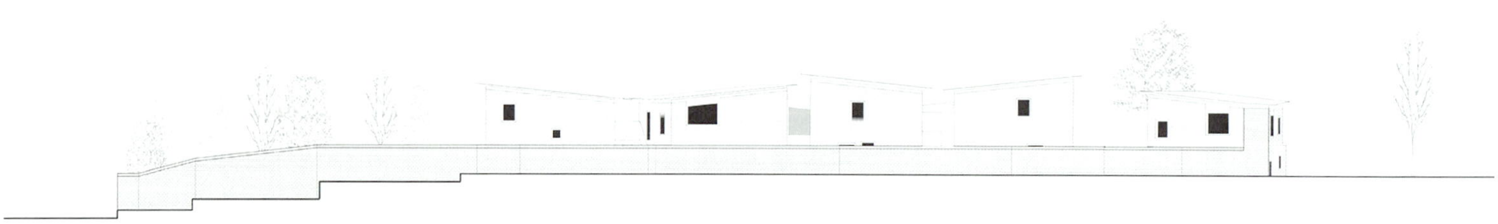

Elevation from the south

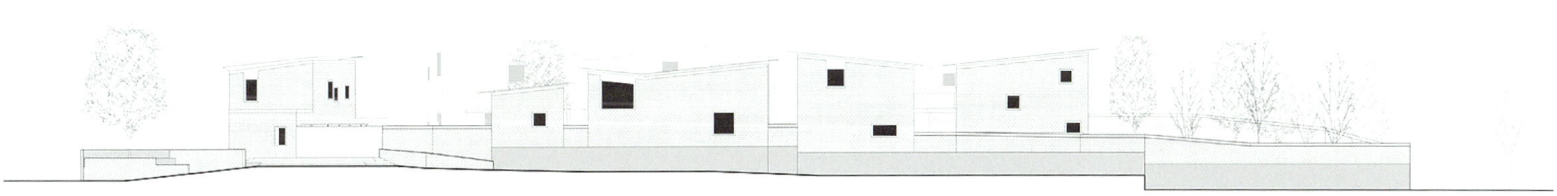

Elevation from the north

Utopia—Library and Academy for Performing Arts

Kees Kaan, Dikkie Scipio and Vincent Panhuysen

PROJECT NAME
Utopia—Library and Academy for Performing Arts

ARCHITECT/S
KAAN Architecten, Rotterdam / The Netherlands

BUILDING PURPOSE
Education, culture

LOCATION
Aalst, Belgium

CONSTRUCTION PERIOD
2016–2018

BRICK TYPE
Facing brick

BRICK AWARD CATEGORY
Sharing public spaces

The very first print of Thomas More's legendary socio-political satire *Utopia* was produced in 1516 on the printing press of the humanist Dirk Martens in the Flemish town of Aalst. Utopia, therefore, is also the name of the new building containing the Aalst City Library and Academy for Performing Arts. The 8,000 square meter complex consists of a former school house from the late 19th century and a minimalist new structure which together form a semi-public space in the city center, surrounded by three small, newly created city squares.

"The complementary long, flat bricks accentuate Utopia's duality."

The so-called "Pupillenschool" was once a school for soldiers' children who received training there before they could join a regiment at the age of 16. It fulfilled various functions over the years, serving lastly as a police station. Like a bookend, it now forms the northeast corner of Utopia. The main entrance is in the new building, between the café and the auditorium. Awaiting visitors inside is an open atrium, dominated by exposed-concrete platforms hanging in the space, with bookshelves and reading tables, the school's decorative exterior façade, and a sculptural concrete staircase. An 11.5-meter-high bookshelf stretches all the way to the roof. A suspended, metal lath ceiling filters the natural light that falls through large glass surfaces and hides the necessary technical installations.

The Academy for Performing Arts occupies the two upper floors on both sides of the atrium. The ballet hall, practice rooms and classrooms in the new building open up towards the city through large window fronts, which, when viewed from the outside, seem to cut into the façade as if by happenchance. Slim, dark anodized metal frames with integrated, external sunscreens reinforce this impression. In the old building, the existing windows were enlarged half a meter downwards, underlining the verticality of the façade structure.

A water-resistant brick named "Rood Aalst" for a dark-red color very common in Aalst was specially developed. To create a contrast to the existing structure, the bricks were designed to be particularly long and flat: They measure 50×10×4 centimeters and give the new building a horizontal effect.

Old and new enter into a successful symbiosis. Although each of them has a recognizable identity, they complement each other at the same time. As a whole, they fit harmoniously into the finely woven context of Aalst. The building, which received a BREEAM Excellent certificate and was erected using local materials, is also convincing in terms of sustainability. 230,000 bricks were recovered during the demolition of the previous building and are to be used elsewhere. [ab]

Entrance front on the south side of the building complex

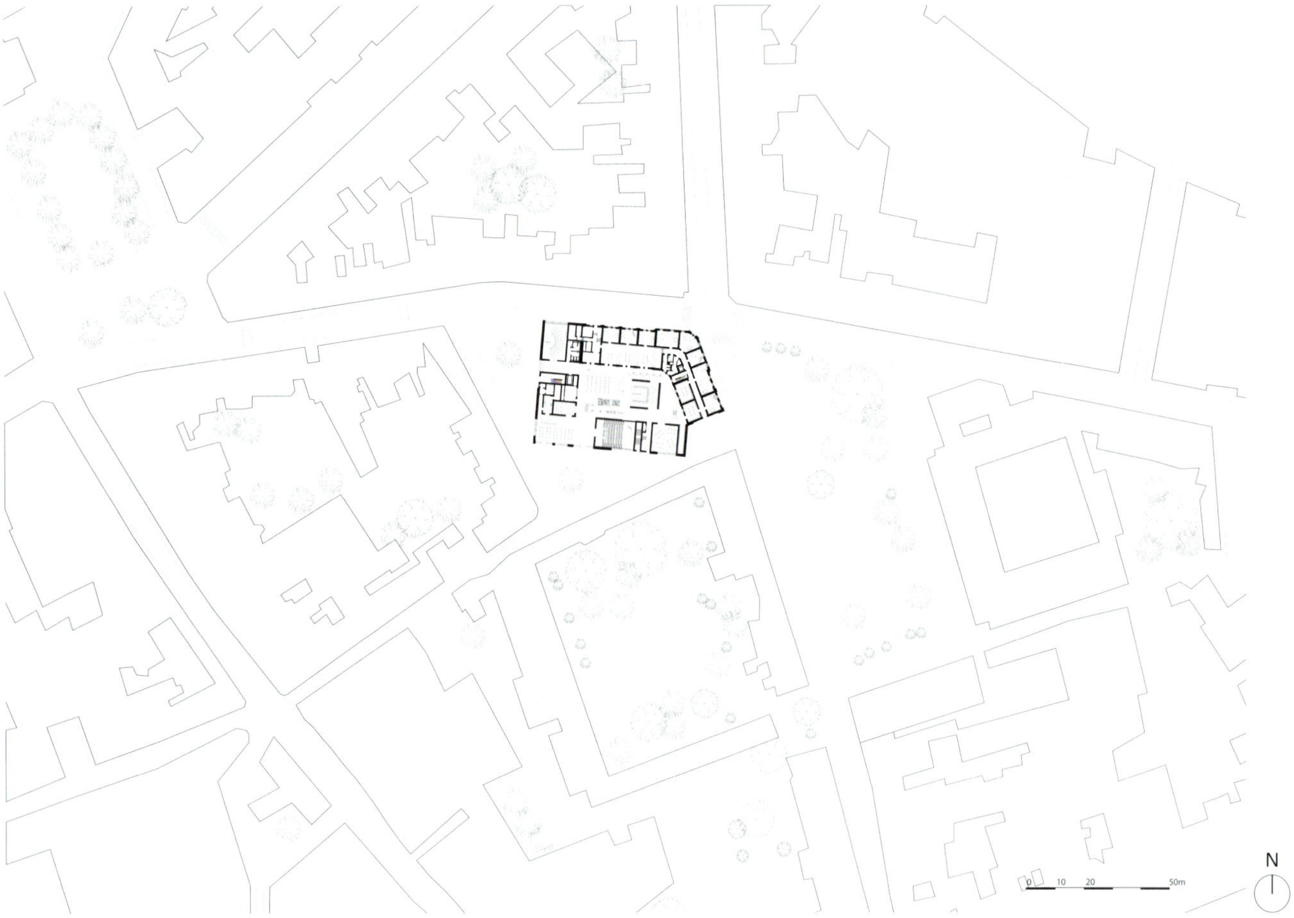

Site plan

The addition connects to the existing building, creating three small squares.

Concrete slabs with bookshelves and reading areas are suspended in the covered atrium.

Street side elevation

MUMA

Storey's Field Centre and Eddington Nursery

Gillian McInnes, Stuart McKnight and Simon Usher

PROJECT NAME
Storey's Field Centre and Eddington Nursery

ARCHITECT/S
MUMA, London/GB

BUILDING PURPOSE
Education, culture

LOCATION
Cambridge, GB

CONSTRUCTION PERIOD
2018

BRICK TYPE
Facing bricks, paving bricks

BRICK AWARD CATEGORY
Sharing public spaces

Eddington is an extension of Cambridge, sited two miles northwest of the English university city and characterized by a family of geometric pale brick buildings including 3,000 new homes and 2,000 bed spaces for post-graduate students, that, taken together and seen from a distance, has something of the air of a fortified town. The university itself has led its development. The rapid growth of Cambridge in recent years has priced young academics and researchers out of the local housing market and yet these are the very people essential to the technological and scientific breakthroughs made in Cambridge tech companies and university laboratories.

"We are fascinated by the richness of possibilities afforded by the humble brick."

Storey's Field Centre and Eddington Nursery are located at the heart of this new town development opposite its ersatz market square and a major green space. This social center takes the form of a group of low-lying, brick-faced buildings clustered around a garden courtyard evoking Cambridge cloisters and college gardens. The main hall, resembling a modern turbine hall, rises above them. This is the community center and arts performance hall. From the outside, it boasts walls of well-detailed brickwork with seats built into the fabric.

Factory-made Dutch stock brickwork has been used imaginatively to add a rich sense of tactility to the building. Bands of vertical stretcher bond brickwork span each entrance and extend around the building to the main hall of the community center, where this is developed as an irregular "strata" of stretcher and soldier course bonds. A vertical ridged pattern of brickwork projects from the façade while, at high level, a band of Flemish bond brickwork featuring projecting, recessed and missing headers gives texture to the façade while also integrating the passive air extract route at the east and west ends of the hall. The striking detail of the brickwork is continued inside the main hall for visual and acoustic purposes: What seems like a contemporary artwork is, in fact, an acoustic screen allowing music, performance, speech and film to work happily in this airy space. The height of the hall assists a passive ventilation system that obviates the need for mechanical ventilation even when the room is full at the height of summer. Special bricks were made for some of the unusual doors, gates, thresholds and windows.

The nursery, or kindergarten building for 100 children features high ceilings and playful "peek-a-boo" windows—circular openings in a brick wall at different heights for small, middling and bigger children—among other childlike elements including a sequence of triangular, square and circular windows that double up as benches, a Moroccan inspired Maghreb gate and "Moongate" doors adopted, a little randomly, from traditional Chinese gardens.

The importance of Eddington and these buildings is twofold. First, this university new town states the case for public spaces and public buildings. These are the heart of any traditional town and the elements that are often missing in new housing schemes by conventional house builders and property developers. Second, the materials employed here are done so intelligently, skillfully and honestly unlike typical new housing developments, especially in 21st century England. Eddington might not be to everyone's taste, yet it speaks of concerned thinking and high quality construction. [jg]

The front wall of the main hall is textured not only for aesthetic reasons, but for acoustic ones as well.

The kindergarten playground with a view to the main hall

KIENTRUC O

Chuon Chuon Kim 2 Kindergarten

Anni Le and Dam Vu

PROJECT NAME
Chuon Chuon Kim 2 Kindergarten

ARCHITECT/S
KIENTRUC O,
Ho Chi Minh / Vietnam

BUILDING PURPOSE
Education

LOCATION
Ho Chi Minh, Vietnam

CONSTRUCTION PERIOD
2015–2016

BRICK TYPE
Clay blocks,
facing bricks, roof tiles,
paving bricks

BRICK AWARD CATEGORY
Sharing public spaces

Rarely has one ever seen a building that uses bricks in so many different ways and as such a matter of course. Single bricks sometimes stand out more, sometimes less; some are occasionally left out of the composite, so that individual small openings in the roof or in the wall result; sometimes a lattice structure evolves out of this principle. Bricks are sometimes staggered towards the back in the bond, resulting in a porous, yet closed structure; sometimes they are combined with small openings. There is something to discover at every corner of the upwardly spiraling small town, which seems to consist of houses stacked on top of one another on a narrow plot—that's how the curiosity of the children for whom this wonderful house was built should be stimulated. It should look as if it were made of Lego bricks, the architects said.

The Kientruc O office in the Vietnamese capital already realized a kindergarten with a similar concept. This time they not only went further skywards, but used bricks as a means to combine a myriad of stimulating structures. Nevertheless, the ensemble does not disintegrate into single pieces. Brick not only serves to maintain the balance of diverse structures, the lively play of light and shadow and a uniform appearance. Its use in this way also serves to naturally ventilate the house.

This variety of spaces and structures is not limited to the surface. There are different room heights and the shape of the simple house with a pitched roof as both a positive and a negative form. At the top, the volumes even stick out and are only supported by one strut. The surfaces are painted colorfully in the recesses; an orange, sculptural-looking spiral staircase connects the first floor with the third. Between the first and second floor there is a smaller version of it; at another spot a third staircase leads from below straight to the first floor.

> "We want to use bare bricks to make the building appear like a solid block that is hollow to house the programmatic elements and to give the building a geometrical impression, but porous enough to look soft and friendly from both outside and inside."

Inside, too, the game of shapes, colors and materials continues. Wood, bricks, colored walls, an open spiral staircase, a yellow barrel roof, round openings, plants, balconies, terraces—in a sparkling fantasy, the architects arranged groups and function rooms around a central core with play areas, which may also at times be allowed to radiate a calm atmosphere. Otherwise, this kindergarten is like an oasis of laughter and bubbling life that breaks out from the regularity of everyday life. And this notion of breaking out of the usual logic is even found in the use of the brick: At the top the outer wall is closed, almost smooth; going downwards it appears to dissolve, to be lighter, to have to carry less, while the spaces above inspire the imagination like in a tree house. [ch]

The continuous use of brick visually links the various volumes.

Winding staircase between the first and third floors

Section

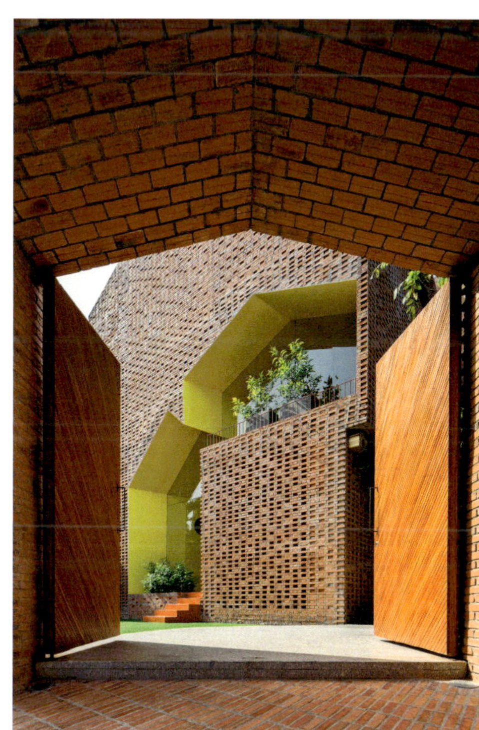

MAX DUDLER

City Library Heidenheim

Max Dudler

PROJECT NAME
City Library Heidenheim

ARCHITECT/S
Max Dudler, Berlin / Germany

BUILDING PURPOSE
Culture

LOCATION
Heidenheim an der Brenz, Germany

CONSTRUCTION PERIOD
2015–2017

BRICK TYPE
Facing bricks, pavement bricks

BRICK AWARD CATEGORY
Sharing public spaces

It is really a small jewel that opened in Heidenheim's city center last year. Hard to believe it, but the new city library replaces a penal institution that had stood here until recently on a plot of land between small-scale structures, the old town and larger post-war buildings.

> "Against the 'skin and bones' of modernity, we have always positioned the idea of the monolithic. A form that is body and shell, construction and texture, cladding and, at the same time, supporting structure. Urban space and architectural space, as we understand it, exist only as a dialogue of such bodies. The brick is an ideal material in this understanding."

The task, therefore, entailed finding a form that can establish a connection between these two different urban fabrics. Moreover, the main piece of property had its pitfalls: it is long and narrow. The Max Dudler architectural office, which had won a two-phase competitive bidding process, responds with a jagged, porous large form that mediates excellently between the various sides and accommodates the different construction heights. Marked at the ends by head buildings towering up to 20 meters, the new library carries the city forward and complements it in terms of its structure with an urban promenade on the east side, which opens obliquely and diagonally out to the city hall in a square on the south side. The building can thus be read in two ways: as a small-scale continuation of inner-city development and as a sculptural body.

The urban structure is taken up, without denying that this is a new and coherent entity that has been implanted. Irregularly punctuated with different-sized windows and enriched by perforated surfaces, the façade is characterized by two different formats of sand-colored, waterstruck clinkers that function in an equally self-contained and supple way in an urban context and effectively promote the dialogue between the houses from different eras.

While the colorfulness of the brick makes reference to Hellenstein Castle, which sits enthroned above the center of the city, the hand-crafted waterstruck brick gives rise to a play of lighter and darker shades on the façade. The irregular shape of the brick and the freestyle bonding provide for a greatly varied and lively façade.

Supplemented by the district media center, the city archives and a café, a house for the municipality has actually been created. The library area extends across the entire second floor as a column-free spatial continuum. This enfilade-like room atmosphere is matched by the choice of materials: white walls, a terrazzo floor and oak accents appropriately bring space and media to full effect. The diverse room heights, the large open stairwell and the sometimes surprising views of the neighborhood make it easy to forget that the long, narrow lot could have been a necessity—instead it has become the virtue of a welcoming house. [ch]

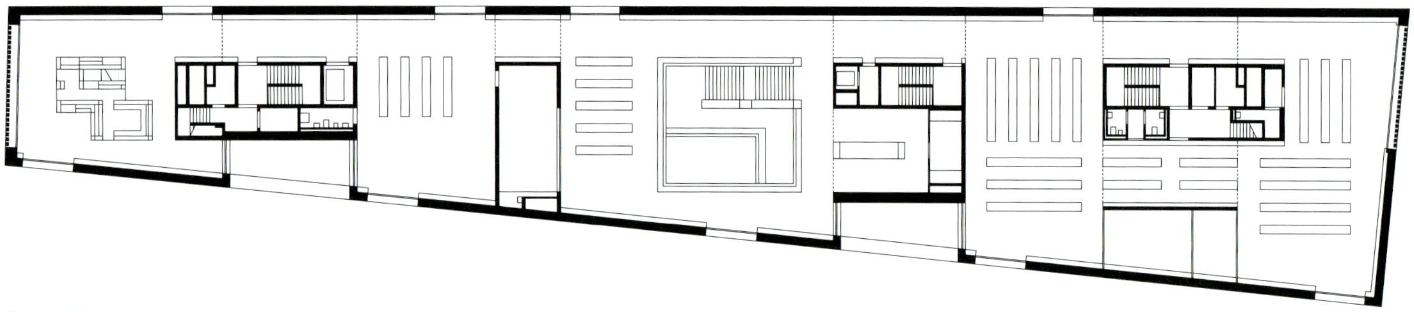

Second floor

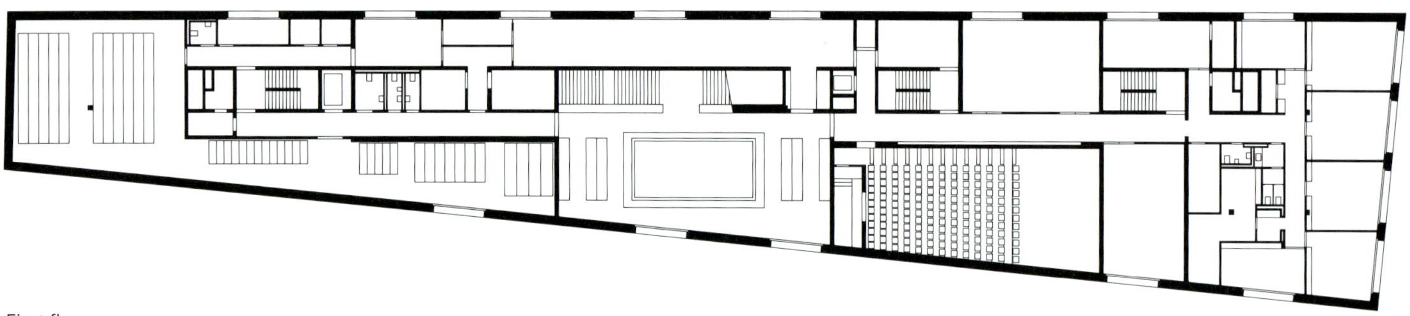

First floor

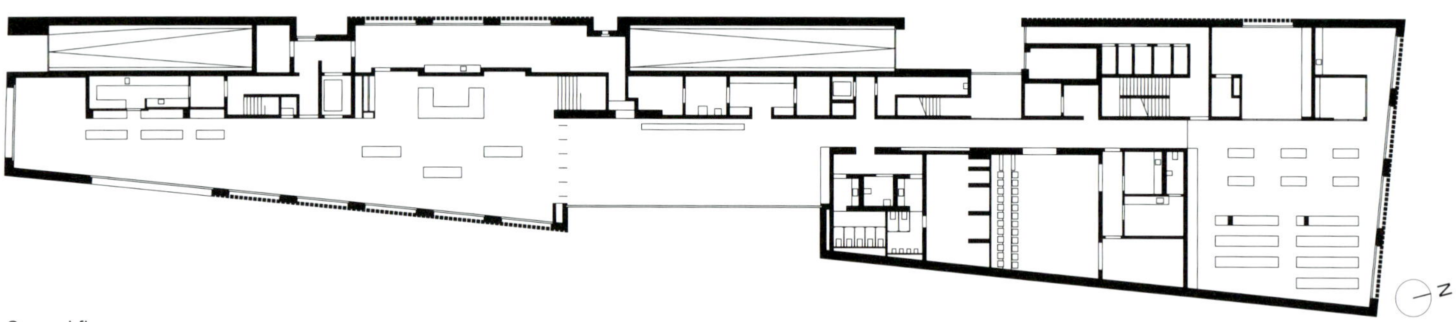

Ground floor

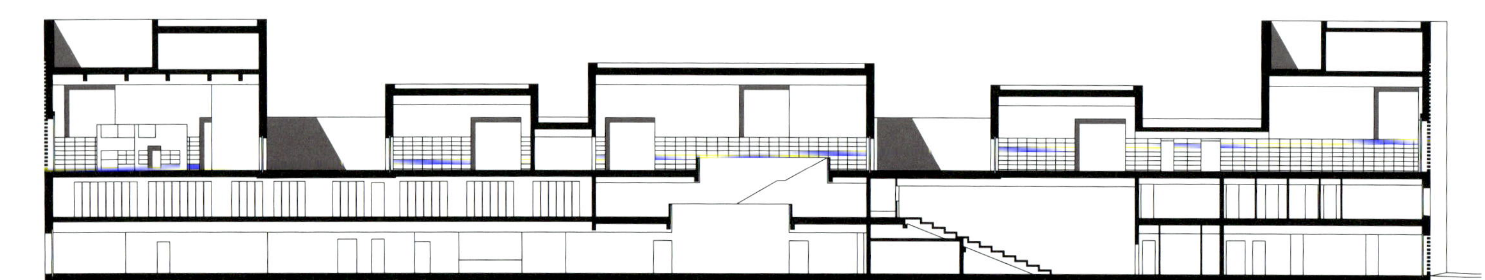

Longitudinal section

The two head buildings are the highest building sections in the row.

B-ARCHITECTEN

Depart

Sven Grooten, Evert Crols and Dirk Engelen

PROJECT NAME
Depart

ARCHITECT/S
B-architecten, Antwerp/Belgium

BUILDING PURPOSE
Culture

LOCATION
Kortrijk, Belgium

CONSTRUCTION PERIOD
2016–2017

BRICK TYPE
Facing bricks

BRICK AWARD CATEGORY
Sharing public spaces

For over twenty years, the transformation of the once-unattractive riverbank zones along the Leie River has been going on in the West Flemish town of Kortrijk. Among other things, new bridges that make formerly isolated areas in the city accessible are being built. One of these bridges opens up an old industrial area along the railway tracks to the west of the city center, the backbone of which is formed by a more than 100-meter-long complex of shed-roofed warehouses. The old halls now house an evening school, offices for start-up companies, and the youth center Tranzit. A new head building for the Depart multipurpose hall completes the ensemble.

"Depart is no-nonsense and efficient, making it a mecca for the man of the crowd."
(Koen Van Synghel, De Standaard)

Originally, the multi-purpose hall was also to be situated in the warehouses, but their ceiling heights were too low and an acoustic insulation of the old building would have become very complex and expensive. They therefore decided to build a new extension at the end of this row of halls which carries on the sawtooth motif of the shed roofs. The series of uniformly dimensioned roofs of the old building now includes a roof distorted in height and width; its shape and dimensions are matched to the function of the spaces below. The loading dock and the cantilever roof of the old building find a continuation in the new building as well.

Located in the northernmost hall of the old building, the Depart foyer can be coupled with the neighboring youth center if required. A metal-clad recess in the façade of the new building directs visitors to the entrance door. Between the foyer and the new structure is an acoustic lock; the large hall with a balcony is behind it. Unlike most venues, it has windows that are hidden behind open brickwork. As a result, it is not a black box, but also offers quality of stay during the day. The same applies to the smaller hall on the first floor, which features windows with acoustic glazing and maintains a visual link to the large hall. Thanks to these openings, the rooms are surprisingly inviting, despite the vandal-proof materials made of concrete and wood wool insulation plates.

Like those of the old building, the façades of Depart were built of red, monk-bonded brick. One sees the similarities between old and new at first glance, but upon closer inspection the differences are striking: The red of the brick is more intense and even; its size is slightly larger than that of the old bricks. The intense terracotta color provides a clear contrast to the exposed concrete of the base, the cantilever roof and the roof edge.

What results is a new building that is both a continuation and a reinterpretation of the existing stock and manages the feat of integrating and setting apart at the same time. [ab]

Instead of implementing the multi-purpose hall in the warehouses, an addition was erected as a continuation and reinterpretation of the existing structure.

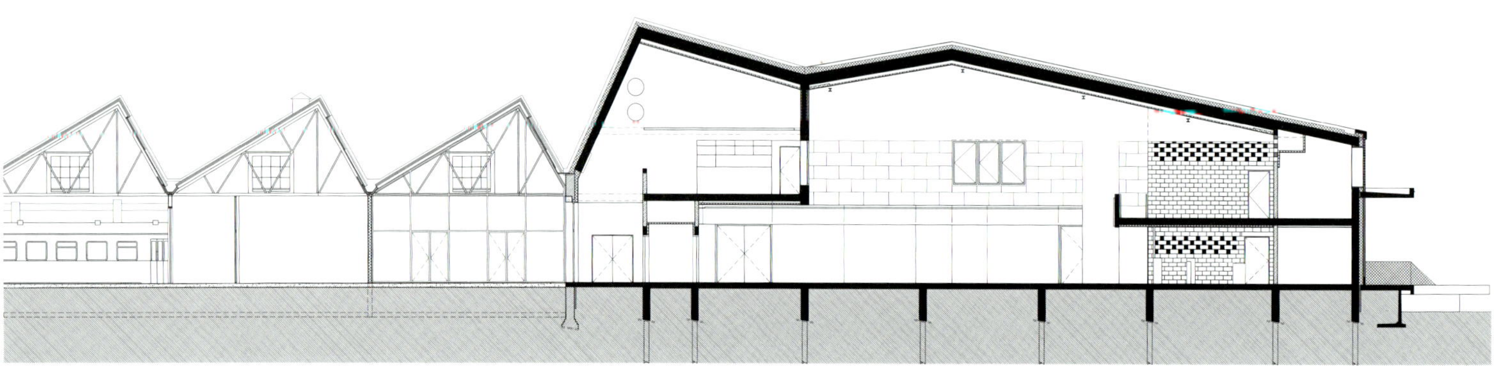

Longitudinal section

Sharing public spaces

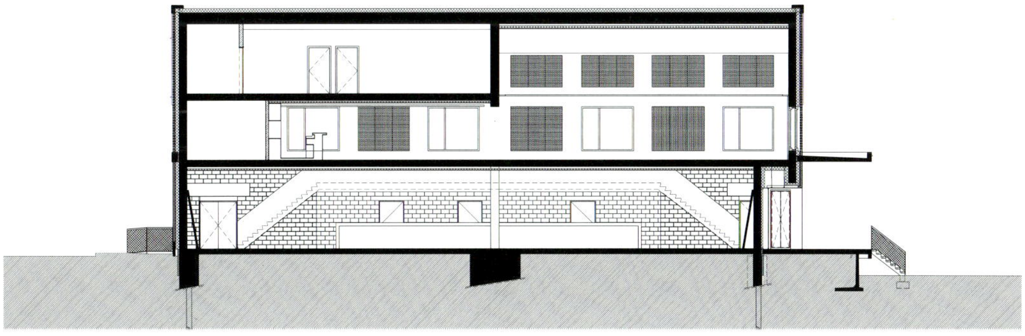

Cross section

WANDEL LORCH ARCHITEKTEN

Renovation and Extension of the Church of the Resurrection Überlingen

Andrea Wandel and Wolfgang Lorch

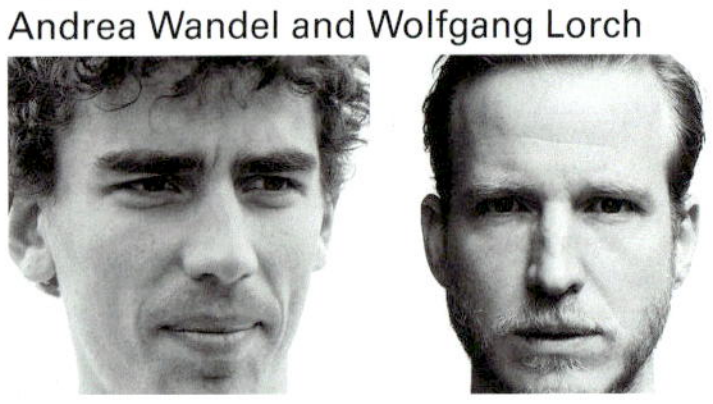

Florian Götze and Thomas Wach

PROJECT NAME
Renovation and Extension of the Church of the Resurrection Überlingen

ARCHITECT/S
Wandel Lorch Architekten, Frankfurt am Main/ Germany

BUILDING PURPOSE
Sacred building

LOCATION
Überlingen, Germany

CONSTRUCTION PERIOD
2016–2018

BRICK TYPE
Clay blocks, paving bricks, glass bricks, roof tiles

BRICK AWARD CATEGORY
Sharing public spaces

Built in 1867, the Auferstehungskirche (Church of the Resurrection) occupies the site of a former Franciscan monastery as a single-nave, neo-Gothic structure on the edge of the city center, just about one hundred meters from the shores of Lake Constance. Since then, it has been rebuilt several times and supplemented by an aisle that disturbs the proportions of the space. In terms of design as well, the alterations had been less than fortunate. Emerging structural damage was a welcome occasion to lend the church more presence in the cityscape and its interior new attractiveness as a space for music, community and worship. The Wandel Lorch architectural office prevailed in the competition. Their concept entailed demolishing the existing portal façade and replacing it with a new one that extends the nave by a good deal. In this way, a small vestibule for the visitors was able to be created inside and a barrier-free restroom integrated. An elevator was added to the extended gallery and now ensures that the longitudinal orientation of the church is strongly emphasized again. Clearly withdrawn compared to the previous design and framed laterally by a wall, a new staircase overcomes the difference in height to the square.

The new façade fulfills the expectation of the church's increased presence in the urban space, without having to attract attention by exaggerated or superimposed effects. A central pointed arch window above the entrance is set back from the outer façade level; the surfaces between the outer edges of the church and this window have been pulled inwards and thereby repeatedly curved, resulting in a slight funnel shape that leads to the portal. Whitewashed bricks are laid in such a staggered fashion that lines following the roof crown and rough, shimmering surfaces arise. Areas are effectively enlivened by plays of light and shadow—the façade faces south—without losing their clear geometric character. The pointed arch is alternately laid with clinkers and glass bricks, so that it seems like a window and like a part of the façade wall. A surface of simple cross ornaments resulted, a calm and at the same time powerful gesture that remains present inside.

"The design of the new portal takes up the traditional characteristics of church portals and transforms them into a contemporary architectural language. The solid clinker bricks made a modern interpretation of the portal possible: It spans out three-dimensionally and guides the visitor inwards."

As the church is also used for concerts, the gallery in the side aisle was removed to accommodate an organ and space for the choir and musicians. During the service, however, the space is clearly realigned, also functionally, on its longitudinal axis. Much value was placed on a uniform effect of the bright white space in the interior, too; old profiles were re-exposed or replicated to make the spatial structure tangible. Both inside and outside, traditional elements and their reinterpretations find their way to each other in a relaxed manner. [ch]

The lattice field closed with glass blocks above the entrance is arched inwards.

Elevation from the southwest

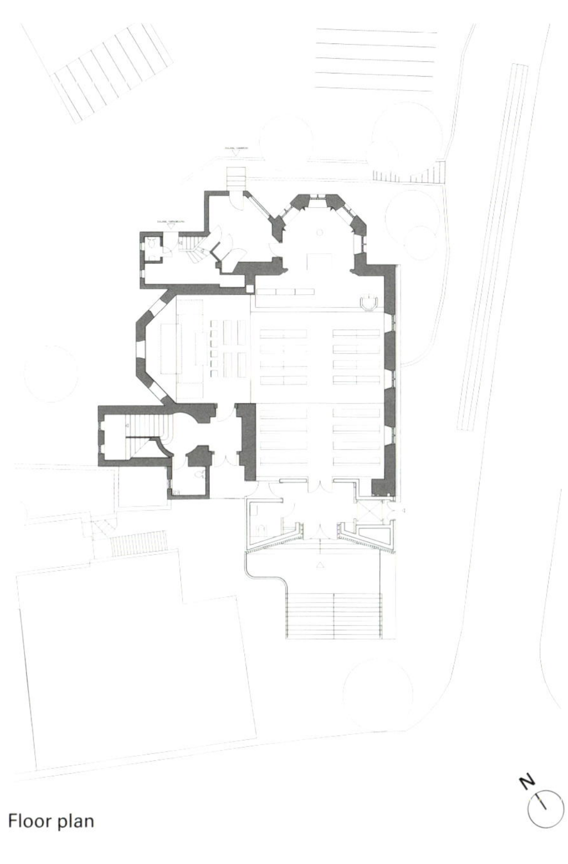

Floor plan

Building outside the box

HUBERTUS ADAM

Stone Made of Fired Clay

Hubertus Adam

Clay is the elementary raw material par excellence: earth, water, fire and air all interplay in its processing. When fired, the material undergoes a process of transformation—soft becomes hard, liquid becomes solid, malleable becomes rigid. Clay is available nearly everywhere. Comparatively easy to work with, it therefore found use in almost all cultures and at all times. Thanks to its durability, ceramics serve archeology as a dating aid. Shards of vessels survive the ages and bear witness to the past, even where written tradition is absent and organic materials have long since disintegrated.

> "Brick is one of the most important construction materials, and this also applies across cultures and epochs."

Not only can clay be processed into receptacles or sculptures, but also into bricks. It is pressed into molds and then fired. All of this can be done by hand and on site, as is still common in some rural areas of the world today. Since the 19th century, however, the process has been highly industrialized. Brick is one of the most important construction materials, and this also applies across cultures and epochs. In a sense, it is the smallest basic module of building. As indisputable as the role of the brick as a material for the shell has always been, so much have the answers to the question of brick façades changed. Sometimes a natural stone façade was perceived as more representative and protective; sometimes a painted plaster surface was desired—in classicism, for instance, with its preference for bright plaster façades. Against this background, the revolutionary character of Schinkel's Building Academy in Berlin becomes obvious: At the height of Prussian Classicism, its most important exponent realized a brick-built structure in the center of the city that was entirely based on the logic of the fired clay. The architect was inspired by industrial buildings in England. Not without reason is the Building Academy, in which frugal terracotta ornaments trace the tectonic structure, sometimes considered as the first modernist building, as a prototype of modular and serial construction, so to speak.

The increasingly industrial character of the building material, which seemed to be losing its artisanal origin, met with criticism from reform architects of the 19th century. Industrially produced machine bricks, glazed shaped bricks and facing clinkers became the targets of a critique of decadence; "liveliness" was called for instead. In a book about brick buildings published in 1910, Albrecht Haupt, who taught at the Technical University of Hannover, detected a certain "brick fatigue." And one of the most important propagandists for a new type of brick architecture, Hamburg's building director Fritz Schumacher, spoke of "dead brick dresses." A major proponent of reform architecture around 1910, he saw the brick as the ideal combination of sensual surface and abstract form and the firing process as the central transformation that not only makes the brick hard and weatherproof, but also gives it a vividly colored surface. Hamburg featured a rich tradition of brick construction, ranging from Gothic churches to the Speicherstadt warehouse district, realized a few years before Schumacher took office. The latter is now part of the UNESCO World Heritage Site and a tourist attraction of the first order. However, with its decorative neo-gothic façades made of glazed clinkers, it became an image of the enemy among reformist architects of the period after 1900, because the perfect industrial bricks lacked the desired surface vividness. In accordance with the demand for material justice advocated by the Deutscher Werkbund, Schumacher and his reform-oriented contemporaries preferred to use hand-formed, waterstruck bricks—so-called "Handstrich-klinker"—and those with production-related irregular surfaces.

Likewise noteworthy in this context is a manifesto titled "Ton. Ein Aufruf" ("Clay – A Manifesto"), written by the sculptor and architect Paul Rudolf Henning in 1917 and published in 1919 as a pamphlet by the Arbeitsrat für Kunst (Workers' Council for Art), founded in the spirit of departure after the First World War. Henning described the advantages of clay and campaigned for its more intensive use. Not only did he see the material extracted from the earth as a material for original, "spiritually transfused" sculptural objects, but also regarded clay as the building material of the future. Colored glazed ceramics, he believed, could save humanity from the "deadly gray-on-gray of the cities." Whether Henning's visionary hopes have been fulfilled is an open question, but the 1920s were a historically important phase for building with ceramic materials at any rate. On the one hand, this involved the production of molded elements and glazes: Technological advances made it increasingly possible to realize special shapes and large formats. Ceramic companies set up special departments for building ceramics—in addition to their vessel, wall tile or brick production. On the other hand, in the context of Expressionist architecture, attempts were made to merge architecture and sculpture, and building with bricks offered rich possibilities. Architects such as Bernhard Hoetger, Fritz Höger and Hans Poelzig took advantage of the possibility of ornamentally structuring the façades of the buildings with protruding and receding bricks. Moreover, attempts were made to construct sculptural clinker brickwork on a building-sized scale.

> "It is the adaptability for different contexts, indeed its universality, which distinguishes the brick."

Of course, structures continued to be built with brick. But in a tightly reined modernism relying more on steel, glass and concrete, it was no longer in the focus of interest. This has changed in the recent past. Interesting is the fact that potentials that had already been debated—and used—by architects of the early 20th century have proven to be fruitful. The frequent use of hand-formed, waterstruck clinkers and misfired bricks aimed at giving the façade a lively expression is striking. Even the ornamentation developed from the rhythm of the brick has returned and been given a new dynamism through digital fabrication processes. Robot-constructed brick walls, on which patterns of different sizes are generated by rotating the bricks, are to be pointed out here. The architects Fabio Gramazio and Matthias Kohler have dealt with this topic in Zurich; a Chinese example is the Shanghai-based architect Philip F. Yuan with his office Archi-Union. To some extent, because of their identical shape, bricks act like pixels, proving that completely new aspects can be gained from a classic building material in the digital era. It is the adaptability for different contexts, indeed its universality, which distinguishes the brick. The Pritzker Prize winner Wang Shu also realizes ornamental brick façades, but associatively ties into the Chinese building tradition and often uses recycled material from demolished historic structures—this is also possible with brick. Returning to a simple design is the goal of Indian-born architect Anupama Kundoo, who also uses partly recycled brick. Low tech, not high tech, is their motto. Green high-tech architecture reinforces the segregation of Indian society due to the costs and the elaborate production technology, says the architect. Therefore, low-cost structures made from local and simple building materials, where the inhabitants themselves could lend a hand, are the order of the day. As said: Clay is simply an elementary material—and always good for innovation in technology, function and design.

KUKA

SAMEEP PADORA & ASSOCIATES

Maya Somaiya Library

Sameep Padora

PROJECT NAME
Maya Somaiya Library

ARCHITECT/S
Sameep Padora & Associates, Maharashtra/India

BUILDING PURPOSE
Education

LOCATION
Kopargaon, India

CONSTRUCTION PERIOD
2018

BRICK TYPE
Facing bricks

BRICK AWARD CATEGORY
Building outside the box

BRICK 20 Category Winner

The Maya Somaiya Library—a radical new building for the Shri Sharda English Medium School at Kopargaon, Maharashtra—occupies a narrow strip of land between existing school buildings, farmland and an electricity sub-station. The site might seem unpromising, yet here Sameep Padora and his Mumbai studio have shaped a balletic building that appears to grow naturally and sinuously from the ground. It rises in fluid form to span a single space library before curving back to the ground again.

The complex form of the roof is made and shaped by three layers of shallow—32 milimeter—brick tiles. Held in compression, these form lightweight vaults proving how adventurous contemporary design can be realized in simple and locally sourced materials.

Here, the roof is one and the same thing as the structure of the building. There are no conventional walls or ceilings, nor indeed any traditional dividing line between the ground and the building. The fabric of the library is a seamless whole.

"Alluding to the intuitive impetus that children have towards the landscape," say the architects, "we imagined the library building to be a formal extension of the ground using brick as material for its tactility, availability, as well as its utility as insulation against the strong sun."

The compound curves of this graceful structure have been made possible through a Swiss 3D computer modeling process that has adapted the Tile Arch System patented by Rafael Guastavino in Spain and the United States and thin-shell structures of the Uruguayan architect Eladio Dieste. The result is a beautiful, undulating, 44-meter vault of thin bricks—105,000 of them—held together in compression. The underneath of the vault forms the uninterrupted ceiling of the library. To maintain its purity of form, fans and lighting are worked into the furniture. During the day, sunlight plays through angular glazed walls onto the underside of the vault and across the library's polished stone floor. After sunset, vaults and shelves are bathed and highlighted in subtle electric light.

Designed with the aid of computers and yet hand-crafted, the library treads a fine, calligraphic line between technological wizardry and a sense of what is natural. "Our practice," says Sameep Padora, "questions the nostalgia involved with the static 'museumification' of craft and tradition, as well as the nature of what today comprises the 'regional' in contexts amplified by their place in global and regional networks."

> "We imagined the library building to be a formal extension of the ground using brick as material for its tactility, availability, as well as its utility as insulation against the strong sun."

The structure of the library, meanwhile, is strong enough to be walked over and, even if it were to lose its windows, desks, shelves, fans and lamps, it could serve as a form satisfying landscape art or memorable architectural sculpture. [jg]

The vault was formed with three layers of thin brick and stretches across the whole library.

Jury statement

"The jury awarded this project as the winner of the category 'Building outside the box' as this innovative project is exactly what this prize is about. The project has used bricks in an unconventional way shaping the roof of the library as a floating landscape and a playground for the school and at the same time embracing the library functions. By using historic inspiration from old brick vaults in different parts of the world and designing with sophisticated computer software, this project is expressed by an advanced brick structure. The complex design still remains humble in its simplicity and contextual understanding of the local Maharashtra site. The heavy brick has been turned into a light and elegant surface referring to the warm color of the earth—and has the potential to become an international landmark."

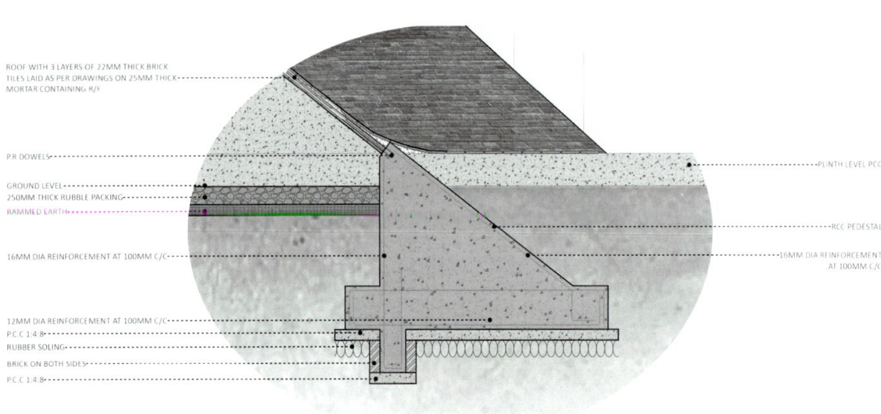

Pedestal detail

The shell forms were calculated digitally, but refer to historic models.

Ventilators and lighting are integrared into the furniture in order to be able to keep the brick vaulting free of infrastructure.

Floor plan

N
S

LIGHT EARTH DESIGNS

Rwanda Cricket Stadium

Tim Hall, Michael Ramage and Ana Gatóo

PROJECT NAME
Rwanda Cricket Stadium

ARCHITECT/S
Light Earth Designs, Cambridge/GB

BUILDING PURPOSE
Leisure

LOCATION
Kigali, Rwanda

CONSTRUCTION PERIOD
2017

BRICK TYPE
Compressed tiles

BRICK AWARD CATEGORY
Building outside the box

BRICK 20 Honorary Mention

This is Rwanda's first cricket pavilion and it is the most memorable expression of the work Light Earth Designs has undertaken for the Rwanda Cricket Stadium Foundation over a number of years. Its aim has been in part to show how the African country can use local and labor-intensive construction techniques in its development programs and in part to demonstrate how a sport like cricket can bring together people of different religions, ethnicities and cultures.

This seriousness of purpose is mitigated by the joyous form of the pavilion designed to reflect the hilly topography of Rwanda and, say its architects, to mimic the parabolic geometry of a high-bouncing cricket ball. The stadium is set in a natural amphitheater with wideopen views of the pitch and of the wetland valley and hills beyond it.

The three masonry vaults spanning changing rooms, an office and a restaurant are a fusion of advanced structural analysis and architectural design, as well as local labor and building techniques. The principal material for the vaults—the largest spans 16 meters and rises to 8 meters—is a thin, air-dried, hand-pressed soil tile that is cheap, easy to make and beautiful. No firing is involved in its making. Tiles are laid on to a geogrid, developed at the University of Cambridge, to give the vaults a degree of seismic protection.

"A building of expressive structural masonry follows the natural flow of forces."

This form of thin-tile vaulting has been used to impressive effect for hundreds of years. In recent history, Antoni Gaudí pushed the technique to new limits, while the Valencian architect Rafael Guastavino took the technique to the United States, where he realized more than a thousand buildings, including the Boston Public Library and New York's Grand Central Terminal. Eladio Dieste, the Uruguayan engineer-architect, advanced brick shell vault construction to previously unheard-of limits, notably with the Iglesia del Cristo Obrero in Estación Atlántida.

Bricks are used to define the edges of the building and spaces within it under the shelter of the arches. Many are laid in a perforate bond allowing breeze and daylight to filter through the pavilion. The bricks have been sourced from high efficiency kilns set up by the Swiss NGO SKAT Consulting that burn low-carbon agro-waste.

"Whilst," according to Light Earth Designs, "the language of the building speaks about progression and dynamism through extreme structural efficiency, the materials speak of the natural, the handmade and the human. The imperfections are celebrated—they are human and beautiful—and, when combined with the layering of natural textures, the building becomes imbued and celebrates this wonderful place." With a single week's training, the local workforce built these daring vaults in just three months. [jg]

Honorary mention:
"The jury commended this project for its structural inventiveness and for its conceptual and social ambition."

The shape imitates a high-flying cricket ball.

The cricket stadium is located at the edge of a natural amphitheater.

BEHET BONDZIO LIN ARCHITEKTEN GMBH & CO. KG

New Administration Building Textilverband Münster

Yu-Han Michael Lin, Roland Bondzio and Martin Behet

PROJECT NAME
New Administration Building Textilverband Münster

ARCHITECT/S
behet bondzio lin architekten GmbH & Co. KG, Münster/Germany

BUILDING PURPOSE
Offices

LOCATION
Münster, Germany

CONSTRUCTION PERIOD
2015–2017

BRICK TYPE
Facing bricks

BRICK AWARD CATEGORY
Building outside the box

The fact that the new building of a textile association should actually represent something textile-like is no big surprise—for the new main office of the Northwest German Textile and Garment Industry in Münster the architects have not been tempted to meet this request with a fabric application or to work with sails and curtains. That would have naturally been possible. But to argue that it could perhaps be much more impressive to give the already prescribed building material of brick a cloth-like effect is a remarkable interpretation of the client's wish after all—and certainly one that people will remember more sustainably.

> "Two things were decisive for the implementation of our design concept: on the one hand, a demanding client who was willing to accompany a research-based design process; on the other hand, the use of digital tools for the development and implementation of a simple design intention that proved complex in detail."

The new office in Münster is the headquarters of the association, where members receive advice on issues such as labor and social policy, the environment and energy, education and further training, as well as consumer protection. The aspiration to have the building also act as a calling card is therefore quite appropriate. That's why the interior decoration was based on textile materials. For example, the lighting is optimized by means of fabric stretched over illuminated ceilings and light strips, complemented in part by large-sized felt objects.

However, the special feature is the textile-like brick façade. The 1300-square-meter surface spans the three-sided, closed structure, which, except for one joint at the structural offset, is only open largely to the north, to the adjoining open space. Through this orientation, all spaces are well-supplied with daylight and do not require sun protection. On one hand, employees can enjoy the full-day view of the countryside in midsummer as well. On the other hand, there are enough areas for the unusual and expressive play on the shape and arrangement of the bricks to enfold on. The architects were inspired by a sculpture of Max Klinger, which shows Beethoven with a scarf draped over his knees that seems light, even though it is made of alabaster. In order to transfer this effect to the façade, a parametric design concept was pursued, whereby the position and shadowing of the bricks are determined in such a way that the impression of a wind-blown cloth is created. Around 74,000 water-struck bricks were laid; one of their sides rotates out of the usual rectangular shape in 2.5-degree increments ranging from 2.5 to 12.5 degrees. This resulted in seven sizes, only one of which is in standard format. The bricks project out of the façade level by up to seven centimeters. Plans that exactly noted the previously calculated position of each brick were drawn up for the construction site. Such an effort is not always able to be made—but it was definitely worth it for this purpose. [ch]

Site plan

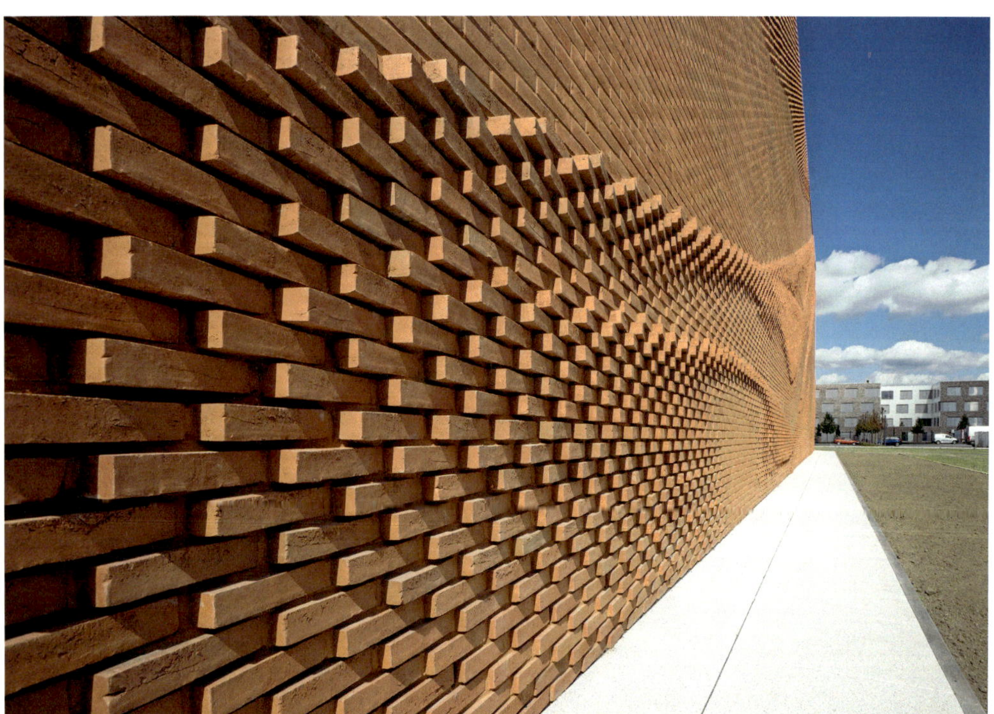

A textile-like impression arises through the placement of the bricks.

The structure is guided across the displacement of the building.

The building opens up towards the north.

ARCHI-UNION ARCHITECTS

Pond Society

Philip F. Yuan

PROJECT NAME
Pond Society

ARCHITECT/S
Archi-Union Architects, Shanghai/China

BUILDING PURPOSE
Culture

LOCATION
Shanghai, China

CONSTRUCTION PERIOD
2016

BRICK TYPE
Facing bricks

BRICK AWARD CATEGORY
Building outside the box

With a history dating back to 1986, the Pond Society is an art platform in Shanghai which organizes exhibitions, workshops and discussions on Chinese and international contemporary art. It is housed in a converted commercial hall on the banks of the Huangpu River in the West Bund art district, on the site of a former airport. The aim of the renovation was to enter into a dialogue with the surroundings while simultaneously finding expression for the art activities inside.

To achieve this, the hall was given a new wooden roof with an exposed truss construction and a distinctive sawtooth shape. The roof was raised at the northern end to enable a gallery to be inserted into the hall, which is illuminated by a large north window. A living area and a storage space are located on the gallery; a meeting room with conference table and a tea kitchen are below it.

While the west wall of the structure adjoins the neighboring building, new façades were placed in front of the south, east and north walls. Made of a greenish-gray, Flemish-bonded brick, they feature an integrated steel reinforcement and alternate between closed and open masonry, so that the walls appear to dissolve more and more as they go upwards. Since many buildings were demolished during the transformation of the West Bund area, the brick material could be reused.

The most striking element, however, is the vaulting in the east façade, which marks the entrance. Its shape results from a force/displacement analysis in combination with stress distribution and wind load tests. The façades were built on site by six-axis robotic arms on mobile platforms. This was decided upon for reasons of economic efficiency, but also served as a source of inspiration for the design: In some parts, the headers stick out of the wall at different lengths, forming not only the arched shape, but also a pixel motif.

> "The maturity of digital tools has inspired us to a new beauty of traditions."

One challenge, though, was to combine modern technology with recycled, artisanal bricks. Since they are not standardized, every single brick had to be scanned by the design team to determine its geometric center as a calibration point for the robot. The end result was anything but a smooth, industrial wall, because the bricks remain irregular around its center. An imperfect wall was ultimately constructed with the precision of robots—and that's precisely what makes the project so appealing. [ab]

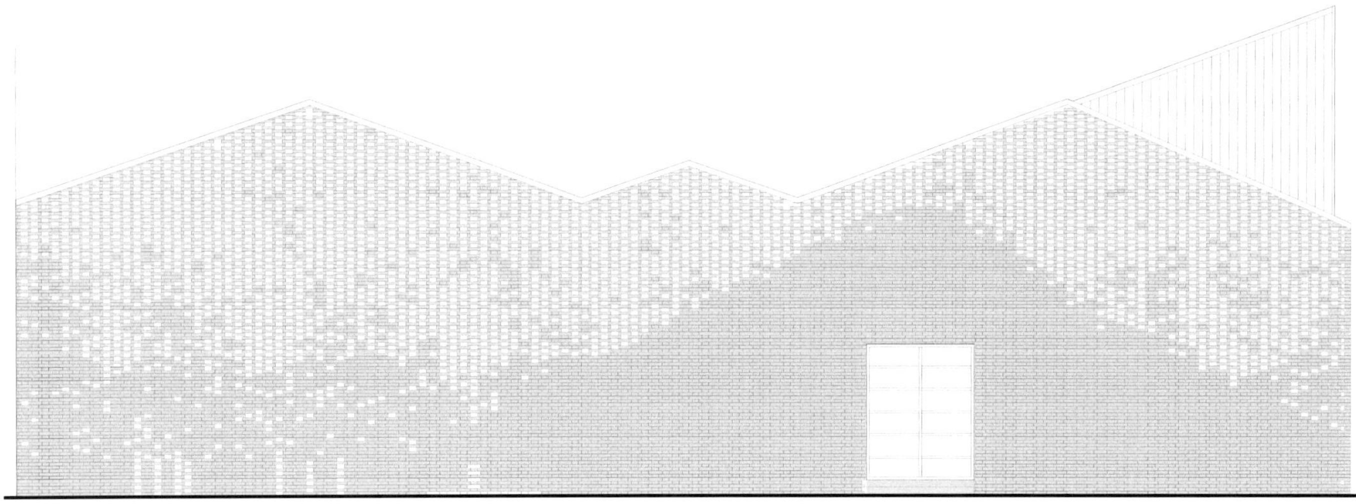

Elevation from the east

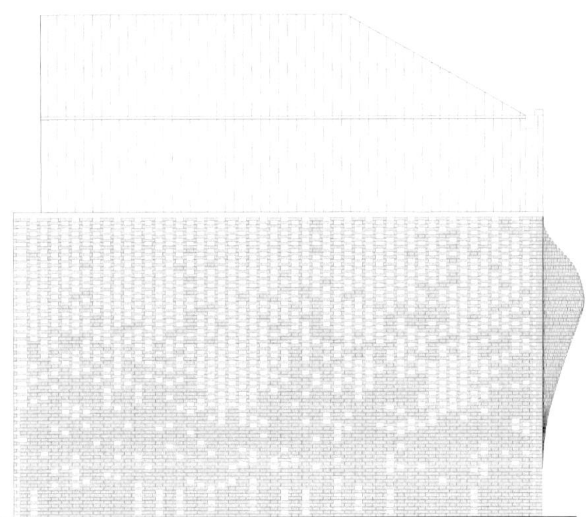

Elevation from the south

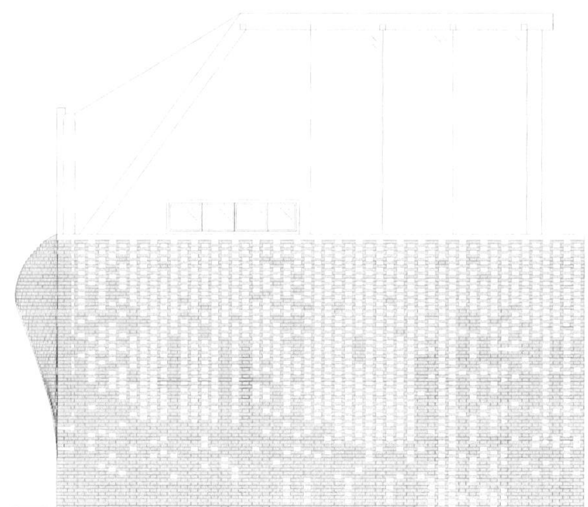

Elevation from the north

The façades were bricked by a six-axis robot arms.

New shapes with traditional materials – in this case with recycled bricks

SUPERTECTURE GUG AND PATRIZIA-KINDERHAUS-STIFTUNG

Nepal School Extension—Fo(u)r Friends

Nadine, Michael, Till, Tobi, Anabella, Phillip, Elek and Angi

PROJECT NAME
Nepal School Extension—Fo(u)r Friends

ARCHITECT/S
Supertecture gUG, Keufbeuren, and PATRIZIA Kinderhaus-Stiftung/Germany

BUILDING PURPOSE
Education

LOCATION
Dhokshang, Nepal

CONSTRUCTION PERIOD
2018

BRICK TYPE
Self-collected facing bricks and paving bricks

BRICK AWARD CATEGORY
Building outside the box

In 2015, more than 7,000 school buildings were destroyed in a major earthquake in Nepal. Since then, many a child has had to take a three-hour walk to reach the next school. That's why the PATRIZIA Children Foundation and the German architect Till Groener decided to expand a small school in the village of Dhokshang by four classrooms with the help of architecture students from the Augsburg University of Applied Sciences. In terms of earthquake resistance, this extension was to consist of four separate buildings to be built by local workers, each with a material from the region: a house made of local sal tree wood, one of rammed clay, one of field stone, one of reused window frames—and one little toilet house made of bricks from buildings that had collapsed during the earthquake.

On site, however, the architects noted that sal tree wood is a rather expensive building material, while the Nepalese bricks lying around everywhere after the earthquake proved to be unexpectedly diverse and beautiful. So they decided to build not just the toilet, but one of the classrooms made entirely of earthquake bricks from Dhokshang and the Kathmandu Valley. They drove through the villages in a truck and asked for brick donations for the school. Although they had initially been warned that no one would give the building material away for free, they succeeded: In total, they collected about 14,000 bricks with more than 50 different patterns, including 200-year-old temple bricks and other one-of-a-kind objects, as well as standard bricks and remaining stock from factories.

> "We wanted to show the world how big the heart of Nepal is."

In the course of the collecting work, the draft for the house gradually took shape. Each façade was designed differently and composed of several masonry surfaces to showcase as many stone variants and bonds as possible. The aim was to mainly use whole bricks and stones; only the south façade is made entirely of rubble and serves as a climbing wall. Shoe shelves, bookshelves and benches are integrated into some of the walls.

To prevent the seepage of rainwater during the monsoon season, the building received a 30-centimeter-high concrete base, above which the three-shelled brick walls rise. Two belts of sal wood in each wall, combined with a post in each corner of the room, serve as traditionally Nepalese, earthquake-resistant reinforcement. The roof structure is made of wood, covered with two different types of roof tiles and decorated at both ends with a typical Nepalese peacock-shaped corner stone: an old brick one, which looks towards the old building, and a new one made of concrete, which looks to the neighboring new buildings.

The jury was "impressed by the material architectural expression of the school by the reuse of tiles and bricks. As a source of inspiration to the design, the reuse has a perspective for sustainable transformation all over the world." [ab]

A classroom made of resued bricks; one made out of rammed clay, one made out of fieldstone and one made out of old window frames.

Floor plan

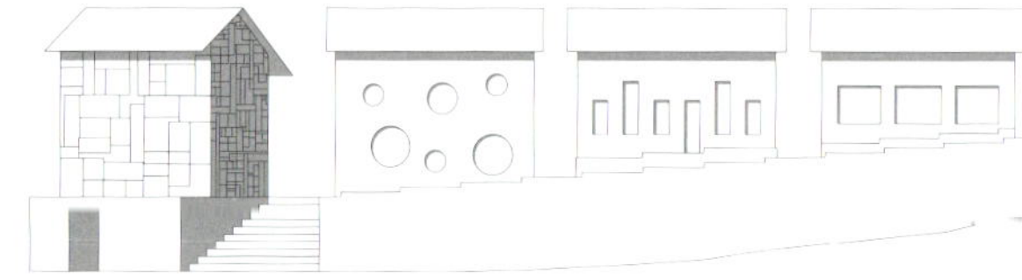

Elevation from the west

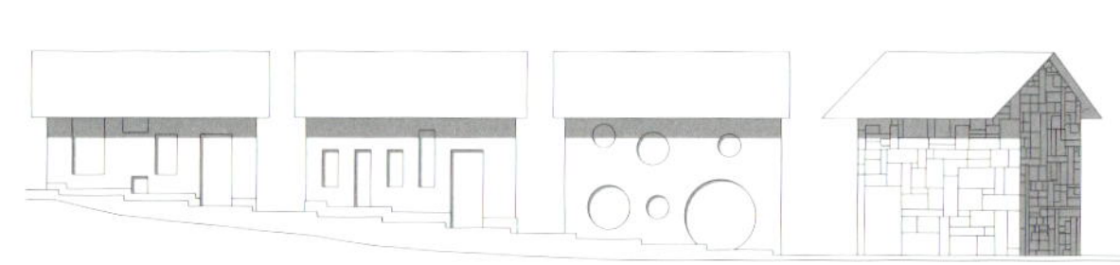

Elevation from the east

Making the school earthquake-proof had the highest priority during construction.

A variety of brick types and bonds were used.

MECK ARCHITEKTEN GMBH

Church Center Blessed Pater Rupert Mayer

Andreas Meck and Axel Frühauf

PROJECT NAME
Church Center Blessed Pater Rupert Mayer

ARCHITECT/S
meck architekten gmbh, Munich/Germany

BUILDING PURPOSE
Sacred building

LOCATION
Poing, Germany

CONSTRUCTION PERIOD
2015–2018

BRICK TYPE
Ceramic façade panels

BRICK AWARD CATEGORY
Building outside the box

Like a shining peak of the snow-capped mountain, the roof of the Blessed Father Rupert Mayer Church Center glistens and sparkles in the light. It stands in a municipality just a few kilometers east of Munich that has grown rapidly in recent years: more than doubling in size since the beginning of the 1990s to over 15,000 inhabitants. Taking this into account, the construction of the new church is intended as a link between the two parts of Poing separated by a railway line: the old core and its expansions, as well as the new residential districts responsible for Poing's growth. Within sight of the train station, where a newly laid-out greenway begins, the striking roofscape of white tiles quite visibly marks the new center of town.

> "Playing with the light in this way, the roof landscape becomes the crystal 'city crown' of the town of Poing."

The church is inspired by Baroque models and their heavenwards-soaring light staging. One of the worldly parts, the one-story plinth, is contrasted by a towering roofscape. The plinth is clad inside and out with the stone typical for the Alpine foothills, the molasse conglomerate. Three upwardly tapering light spaces are spanned across steel girders above a square floor plan. They represent the Trinity and guide the light to places important for the liturgy: From the organ loft one of the roof planes directs the light into the center of the room, the second light accentuates the place of baptism, while the third and—at about 30 meters—highest element of this illuminated architecture brightens the altar and tabernacle. Here the incidence of light is zenithal, while it otherwise enters from the side. The white surfaces of the concrete structure are fully in service to the notion of the spiritual light experience and the differentiating spatial dramaturgy. The fourth segment is kept flat and assigned to the entrance area.

On the outside, the idea of a sparkling crystal was contrasted with the inner light space. With a surface area of about 2,600 square meters, the polymorphic roofscape is covered with 15,000 white tiles manufactured in a mainly artisanal process. On the edge length of 38.7 centimeters, they develop three-dimensionally, similar to an irregular folding plate, to a thickness of 13 centimeters. Due to the white surface glaze, the diverse slants of the resulting surfaces provide different reflection depending on the position of the sun. A precisely elaborated laying pattern that varies the direction of the tiles has ensured that the light is reflected and scattered in a particularly strong manner. They are clamped onto a non-visible steel substructure with offset joints. Through this building, the new center of Poing has truly become one: with a structure that combines technology, tradition and contemporaneity in a fascinating way. [ch]

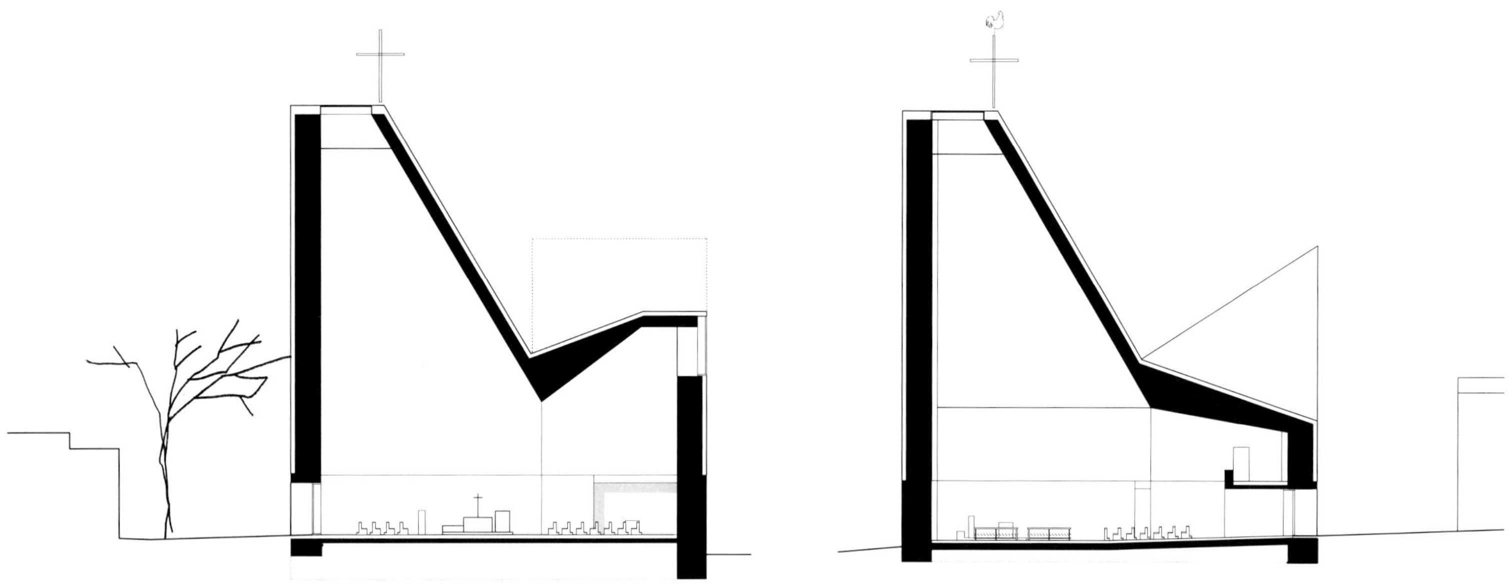

Sections

Model

View to the altar

Thousands of white, three-dimensional tiles cover the exterior of the church.

ESTUDIO BOTTERI-CONNELL

Experimental Brick Pavillion

Sofía Botteri, Patricio Connell,

Rosalía Vicente, Augustín Ichuribehere and Sacha Porcel

PROJECT NAME
Experimental Brick Pavillion

ARCHITECT/S
Estudio Botteri-Connell, Buenos Aires/Argentina

BUILDING PURPOSE
Leisure

LOCATION
La Plata, Buenos Aires, Argentina

CONSTRUCTION PERIOD
2016

BRICK TYPE
Facing bricks

BRICK AWARD CATEGORY
Building outside the box

City Bell is a settlement by the River Plate founded by English immigrants to Argentina, led by George Bell at the beginning of the 20th century. It grew in piecemeal fashion: A railway station with trains to Buenos Aires arrived in 1914, followed gradually by golf and equestrian clubs, a theater, an athletic club and an art gallery. With its tree-lined streets, it became a pleasant southern suburb of Buenos Aires, a green escape from the city for those keen on sports and recreation in the open air.

> "The dynamism acquired with the creation of movable panels of brick, submits the material to an unusual behavior."

The "Experimental Brick Pavilion" suits present-day City Bell quite well. It is comprised of four simple bedroom studios, designed for weekend breaks, secreted behind walls of perforated brick panels. The bricks are held without mortar in steel frames. These frames slide, enabling each studio to open up to the garden it faces. As the frames open and close, the pattern of the façade of the pavilion also changes.

On the other side of the single story pavilion, the studios give way to a corridor lined with a fixed perforated brick screen. This allows for privacy and for daylight to dapple into the corridor. At sunset, electric light shines back through the screen so that the building resembles a large jewel box lit from within. When the screens are closed on the garden front of the pavilion, the same visual effect is realized.

This Pavilion is a beguiling idea that, one day, could be applied to apartment blocks, among other buildings, in cities where sunlight is strong and temperatures high. On a taller building, the patterns played by the sliding brick screens would create façades that, although disciplined by the geometry of the architecture, would be varied during the course of a day.

It is not difficult to see how the design of this experimental pavilion could be applied to high-density student accommodation on college campuses or to low-cost studios for those starting their careers in city centers, both typologies where balance between privacy and sociability is all-important.

The pavilion is also an experiment in dry brick construction. Sofía Botteri and Patricio Connell's work is characterized by a willingness to experiment with traditional and modern materials in the design of, mostly, bespoke family homes. They show that this can lead to houses that are as enchanting as comfortable. [jg]

The envelope of the pavilion consists of self-supporting, steel-encased brick panels in dry mortarless construction.

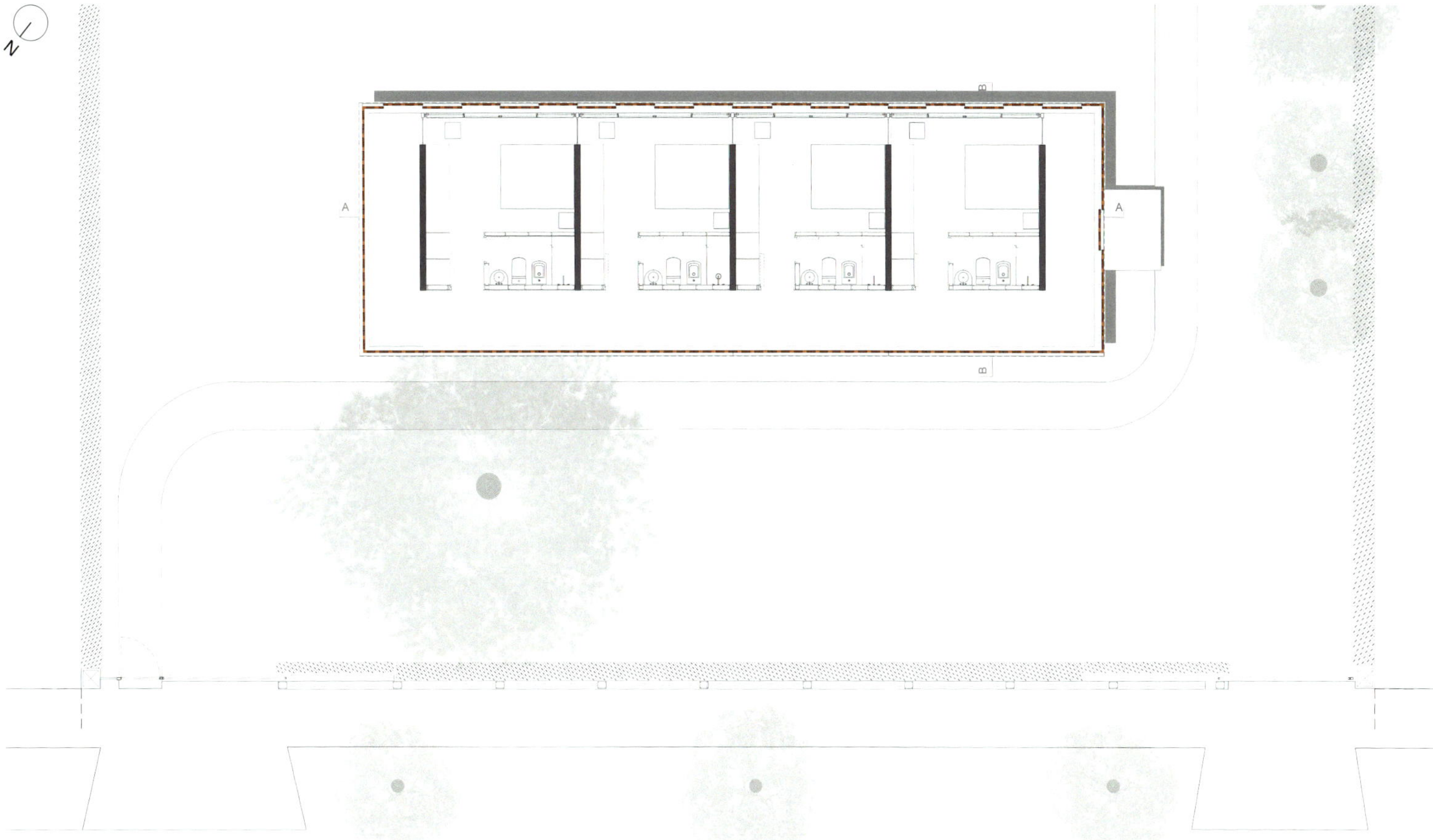

Floor plan

INGENIEURE OHNE GRENZEN E.V.

Initiative Rising Star—School Buildings for Hopley, Zimbabwe

Kristina Egbers

PROJECT NAME
Initiative Rising Star—School Buildings for Hopley, Zimbabwe

ARCHITECT/S
Ingenieure ohne Grenzen e.V., Berlin/Germany

BUILDING PURPOSE
Education

LOCATION
Harare, Zimbabwe

CONSTRUCTION PERIOD
2016–2018

BRICK TYPE
Facing bricks, paving bricks

BRICK AWARD CATEGORY
Building outside the box

Ingenieure ohne Grenzen (Engineers without Borders) is a private aid organization founded in 2003. Their goal is to improve the living conditions of needy and disadvantaged people in the long term. With the ideal of support based on partnership, Ingenieure ohne Grenzen is helping worldwide: to alleviate the consequences of earthquakes in Nepal, to provide drinking water treatment in Africa; the association is also active in the integration of refugees in Germany.

The Rising Star School in the settlement of Hopley, Harare, Zimbabwe came into existence in 2010 on the initiative of the settlement residents. For a long time the children were taught in it under the most primitive conditions: first under tarpaulins and clay shelters, then in rooms that were narrow and poorly lit.

These deficiencies have been removed by the new building. Created on the basis of a diploma design submitted to the University of Stuttgart, it was further developed there with a local project group of Ingenieure ohne Grenzen.

The concept is based on a modular principle. Through the construction of the first seven classrooms, the participants, some of them young, unskilled workers, acquired valuable knowledge that enables them to carry out the remaining stages of construction independently and quickly. Moreover, they are given the much-needed opportunity to earn money; unemployment is very high in the settlement.

Building upon a master plan, a campus for 1,000 pupils with classrooms, administrative spaces, a library and a school garden is to arise by 2020. Settlement residents can also use the spaces for their gatherings. A total of four buildings will eventually be grouped around a courtyard that provides shelter for the children. Three rectangular structures take in four rooms, the fourth will have six. They are combined in groups of two under an elongated roof; covered open spaces lie between them. Arcades connect the classrooms to each other towards the courtyard.

> "There are only a few different brick types, colors and structures. The fact that you can build beautiful and high-quality buildings with this assortment shows that less is often more!"

The material for the approximately 35-centimeter-thick walls consists of fired clay bricks made in a nearby factory. They serve the indoor climate well in both hot and humid times, and the double roof prevents the rooms from heating up. The traditional construction method is implemented in a contemporary architectural language: Planning is based on the fundamental idea of wall slabs, lined up transversely like bulkheads, with large arches. They emerge as wall attachments in the outer wall, in which, like an ornament, the slits necessary for the ventilation of the roof gap are visible. The smaller arches connect inwardly to the large ones of the arcade. The arch motif ensures that the house stands out as the settlement's special building, which the inhabitants can be—and are—proud of.

As the jury asserted: "With a vision to support children with education in Zimbabwe, an architectural statement arises with the Rising Star school created with local knowledge, local craftsmanship and a collaboration with Ingenieure ohne Grenzen e.V. We were impressed by the beauty and structure of the buildings done with very few resources and the impact that architecture can have to stimulate and frame a vision." [ch]

A covered open space lies between two classroms respectively.

The simple, repetitive construction principle enables further construction of the complex by unskilled workers as well.

INTERVAL ARCHITECTS

Tower of Bricks

Yunduan Gu and Oscar Ko

PROJECT NAME
Tower of Bricks

ARCHITECT/S
Interval Architects, Shanghai/China

BUILDING PURPOSE
Culture, leisure

LOCATION
Hengshui, China

CONSTRUCTION PERIOD
2017–2018

BRICK TYPE
Clay blocks, paving bricks

BRICK AWARD CATEGORY
Building outside the box

The dream-like Tower of Bricks rises from a new botanic garden on the edge of the city of Hengshui. Intriguingly, with its observation platform overlooking the botanic gardens, the wetlands and far beyond, it rises from an abandoned brickworks. The arcaded buildings and rooms at the base of the tower were once brick kilns, while the tower itself was originally the brickworks chimney.

> "We decided that the memory and history of the old kiln has to be recalled and remembered with the new architecture."

This strangely romantic building complex is now a cultural and art center with spaces to see and study plant life. With a restaurant, too, this is not a place to hurry. In fact, the Tower of Bricks has something of the air of ancient monastery, especially with its vaulted arcades and central courtyard. And, yet, this was once a large Hoffman kiln, a type of brickworks patented in Germany in 1858 by Friedrich Hoffman.

A Hoffman kiln consists of a main fire passage surrounded on each side by ranges of small rooms containing pallets of bricks. A "fire wagon" drawn along the main passage heats and dries the bricks with hot gases that flow between the rooms. In full action, the kilns were hot, fiery, intensely productive and rather frightening places to be, with the fire sometimes burning continuously for years and even decades.

Interval Architects—the Shanghai studio led by Oscar Ko and Yunduan Gu—have turned the former kiln into a haven of peace. The studio has brought gradations of daylight into the building through various patterns of open brickwork and notably into the internal courtyard. Some of these patterns are as beautiful as they are mesmerizing. The tower itself is clad in regular patterns of open and closed brickwork, too. This adds subtle variety to its essentially monolithic form while encouraging daylight up the stairs to the observation platform.

"The new architecture," say the architects, "is a public facility that contrasts with the old kiln, which was an introverted building purely for industrial production. With the intention to connect to the spatial history of the place, the new botanic art center has a massing and spatial composition that references the old kiln, but is programmed with contemporary functions." One of these functions is, evidently, to delight visitors. [jg]

Diverse brick sizes and bonds for a beautiful, contemplative sequence of spaces

The fomer brickworks is now an art and cultural center; the tower stands on the spot of the old kiln.

Site plan

The authors

HUBERTUS ADAM was born in Hannover and studied art history, philosophy and archeology at the University of Heidelberg.

Since 1992 he has been working as a freelance art, design and architectural historian, as well as an architecture critic for various journals and daily newspapers, especially for the *Neue Zürcher Zeitung.* In 1996/97 he was the editor of *Bauwelt* magazine in Berlin. Moving to Switzerland in 1998, he served as the editor-in-chief of *archithese*, an architecture magazine published in Zurich. From 2010 he was artistic director of the S AM Swiss Architecture Museum in Basel, and its director between 2013 and 2015. Adam has written numerous publications on contemporary architecture and architecture of the 20th century, on photography, art and sculpture around 1900, on design history, landscape architecture, stage design and monuments. He works as a juror as well as a speaker, moderator and guest critic for various international institutions and universities. In 2004 he received the Swiss Art Award in the category of art and architecture education.

ANNEKE BOKERN, born in Frankfurt, Germany, is an architecture journalist and owner of architectural guiding company architour in Amsterdam. She holds an M.A. in Art History from the Freie Universität Berlin and has been living in Amsterdam since 2000. Her publications focus on Dutch architecture and design. Her articles have been published in various German and international magazines, including *Bauwelt, Baumeister, Domus, Topos* and *uncube magazine.* She also contributes to book publications and is currently writing an architecture guide to Rotterdam. With her company architour she organizes architecture tours for groups in the Netherlands.

AGLAÉE DEGROS is professor, chair of the Institute of Urbanism at Graz University of Technology and Science Fellow from the Free University of Brussels. In 2001, she cofounded with Stefan Bendiks Artgineering, an office dedicated to improve the relation between landscape, city and infrastrutcure based in Rotterdam, which moved to Brussels in 2014. Degros has held various teaching positions and visiting professorships at Delft University of Technology, the Rotterdam Academy of Architecture, the Free University of Brussels, the Academy of Fine Arts Vienna, and Vienna University of Technology, among others. She is co-author of *Brussels, [re]discovering its spaces* (2014) and *Traffic Space Is Public Space* (2019). She regularly serves as a jury member at international urban planning and design competitions.

JOB FLORIS is an architect and co-founder of Monadnock, a Rotterdam-based office for architecture, urbanism, interior and research. He obtained his master's degree in architecture from the Rotterdam Academy of Architecture and Urbanism in 2004, following his study of architectural design at the Academy of Fine Arts Sint Joost in Breda. He gained his first professional experience at the architectural firm of Christian Kieckens Architects in Aalst, Belgium. Floris continued to broaden his skills in Flanders by working at Architectenbureau Poulissen & Partners in Antwerp from 1998 to 2000. Subsequently, Floris returned to practice in the Netherlands, working as project architect at Rapp+Rapp until the co-foundation of Monadnock in 2006. He publishes in various architecture magazines and was a member of the editorial board of *OASE Journal for Architecture* from 2008 to 2016. Job served as head of the Masters Course in Architecture at the Rotterdam Academy of Architecture and Urban Design from 2010 to 2018. He has held various visiting lectureships throughout Europe and is currently a guest professor at the EPFL in Lausanne.

JONATHAN GLANCEY is a journalist, critic, curator, author and radio and television broadcaster. An Honorary Fellow of the Royal Institute of British Architects, he writes for the *Daily Telegraph, CNN Style* and the *Architectural Review,* among other publications and websites. He began his career with the *Architectural Review* and was a founding editor of *Blueprint* magazine. From 1989 to 1997 he was the architecture and design editor of the *Independent* and from 1997 to 2012 the architecture and design correspondent of the *Guardian.* His architectural books include *Architecture: A Visual History, Lost Buildings, The Story of Architecture, London: Bread and Circuses* and *Dymaxion Car: Buckminster Fuller* (with Norman Foster).

Among his books on engineering design and history are: *Spitfire: The Biography, Concorde: The Rise and Fall of the Supersonic Airliner, Giants of Steam,* the story of the world's last great steam locomotive engineers, and *The Journey Matters.*

Currently he is researching a book on the links between aviation and architecture and curating a major exhibition of the work of the visionary Hungarian architect Imre Makovecz.

CHRISTIAN HOLL studied architecture in Aachen, Florence and Stuttgart. From 1997 to 2004 he was the editor of *db – deutsche bauzeitung,* and founded frei04 publizistik together with Ursula Baus and Claudia Siegele in 2004, where he published reports, commentaries and essays from 2014 to 2016. Since 2017 frei04 publizistik has been the publisher of the magazine for architecture and urbanism *marlowes.de.* Holl is a book author, works as a freelance editor, journalist and critic, and had teaching assignments in Darmstadt, Stuttgart, Wuppertal, Kaiserslautern and Frankfurt on Main. From 2005 to 2010 he was a scientific assistant at the Urban Design Institute of the University of Stuttgart, from 2007 to 2013 editor of *german-architects.com.* Since 2008 he has been a curator and member of the exhibition committee of the "architekturgalerie am weißenhof," since 2010 managing director of the Association of German Architects Hessen (BDA Hessen).

LAURA ILONIEMI is an architectural publicist working in London. She has written on promoting architecture in many publications, including her book *Is It All About Image?* (Wiley, 2004), and as guest editor of "The Identity of The Architect" in the November/December 2019 issue of *Architectural Design* (Wiley). Iloniemi holds an M.Phil. from the University of Cambridge in architectural history and philosophy in addition to a degree in museology from the École du Louvre and an MA in art history from the University of Edinburgh. Over the years, she has spoken about publicizing architecture and is currently teaching media relations at the Architectural Association in London.

JANA REVEDIN is a German architect, theoretician and writer. She studied architecture and urban planning in Buenos Aires, Princeton and Milan, did her doctorate and habilitation at the University of Venice, and is now Professor of Architecture and Urban Planning at the École spéciale d'architecture Paris. Revedin specializes in the German reform avant-garde, whose social and ecological standards make it the benchmark of contemporary sustainable architecture and urban development. Since 2014, the long-time UNESCO sustainability expert and UNESCO delegate to the Research and Teaching Commission of the International Union of Architects has been a knightess of the honorary French legion of the Chevaliers des Arts et des Lettres. The Global Award for Sustainable Architecture™, created by her in Paris in 2006, is awarded under the auspices of UNESCO. www.revedin.com

The jury

METTE KYNNE FRANDSEN graduated from the School of Architecture of the Royal Danish Academy of Fine Arts in 1987. In 1993, she started working at Henning Larsen Architects and became the company's CEO in 2003. The international bureau has subsidiaries in the USA, Germany, Hong Kong, Norway, the Faroe Islands and Saudi Arabia and employs close to 350 people with more than 30 nationalities. Her work focuses on the creation of living and sustainable architecture. Her most well-known work includes "The Wave" in Denmark and the Eystur Town Hall in Iceland.

She is a member of the Danish Architects' Association and the Artists' Society of the Royal Danish Academy of Fine Arts.

Among other prizes, she was awarded the Mies van der Rohe Award, the AIA International Region Design Award and the Aga Khan Award for Architecture.

TONI GIRONÈS SADERRA was born just north-east of Barcelona and studied architecture at Vallès Architecture University and at Politècnica de Catalunya University, where he received his PhD in Architecture in 2016.

From 1993, the beginning of his professional path, his work was recognized by awards, publications, expositions, among these several FAD awards, the Premi Joves Architects in Catalunya, expositions at the Venecian Biennal, nominations for the Mies van der Rohe Award or the Borromini Award.

His most famous works include the Museum of Climate (Lleida), "80 Social Housing Units" (Salou) or "35 Houses and their Transitional Spaces Towards the City" (Badalona).

HELENA GLANTZ was born in Sweden, where she also completed her post-graduate studies at the Royal Academy of Fine Arts in 1998. After working in various architectural bureaus for 13 years, she started her own bureau in Stockholm in 2001 as founding partner and CEO of UD Urban Design AB.

Her work focuses on the connotation of "design in relation to urbanity." Through the exploration of cities and their inhabitants' connection to technical support systems, Urban Design was able to create a broad collection of work ranging from offices, housing and brand identity to the design of technical facilities.

Besides receiving a Wienerberger Brick Award 2018 in the category "Building outside the box" for Värtan Bioenergy CHP-plant, Helena Glantz and her team have been awarded and shortlisted for several other awards such as the Mipim Award or the American Architecture Prize.

TINA GREGORIČ was born in Slovenia, where she studied at the Faculty of Architecture of the University of Ljubljana. She finished her postgraduate studies with distinction in 2002 at the Architectural Association in London. Since then, she has worked with Zaha Hadid Architects in London, taught at the AA and the TU Graz. In 2003 she founded Dekleva Gregorič Architects together with her partner Aljoša Dekleva in Ljubljana. In 2014 she became professor of architecture and head of department at TU Wien.

The work of Dekleva Gregorič Architects pursues the concepts of "research by design" and "design by research". With this approach, the office has been nominated for the Mies van der Rohe Award several times, was awarded the Wan House of the Year 2015 Award and the International Architecture Award 2012, just to name a few.

Their most well-known projects include the University Campus Livade 1.0 in Izola, Slovenia, "XXS House" in Ljubljana, and the "Clifftop House" in Maui, Hawaii.

JONATHAN SERGISON was born in St. Asaph, UK. He graduated from the Architectural Association in London in 1989 and gained professional experience working for David Chipperfield and Tony Fretton. In 1996, he established Sergison Bates architects in London with Stephen Bates. Jointly responsible for the design direction of the practice Jonathan now leads the Zurich studio, which opened in 2010.

Sergison Bates focus on urban planning, public buildings and housing and are currently involved in a wide range of projects in the UK and abroad. Sergison has taught at a number of architecture schools, including the Architectural Association in London, the Swiss Federal Institute of Technology (ETH) in Zurich, and the Graduate School of Design at Harvard University.

Several of their projects have received awards and the practice's work has won international recognition with the Heinrich Tessenow Medal and the Erich Schelling Medal for Architecture.

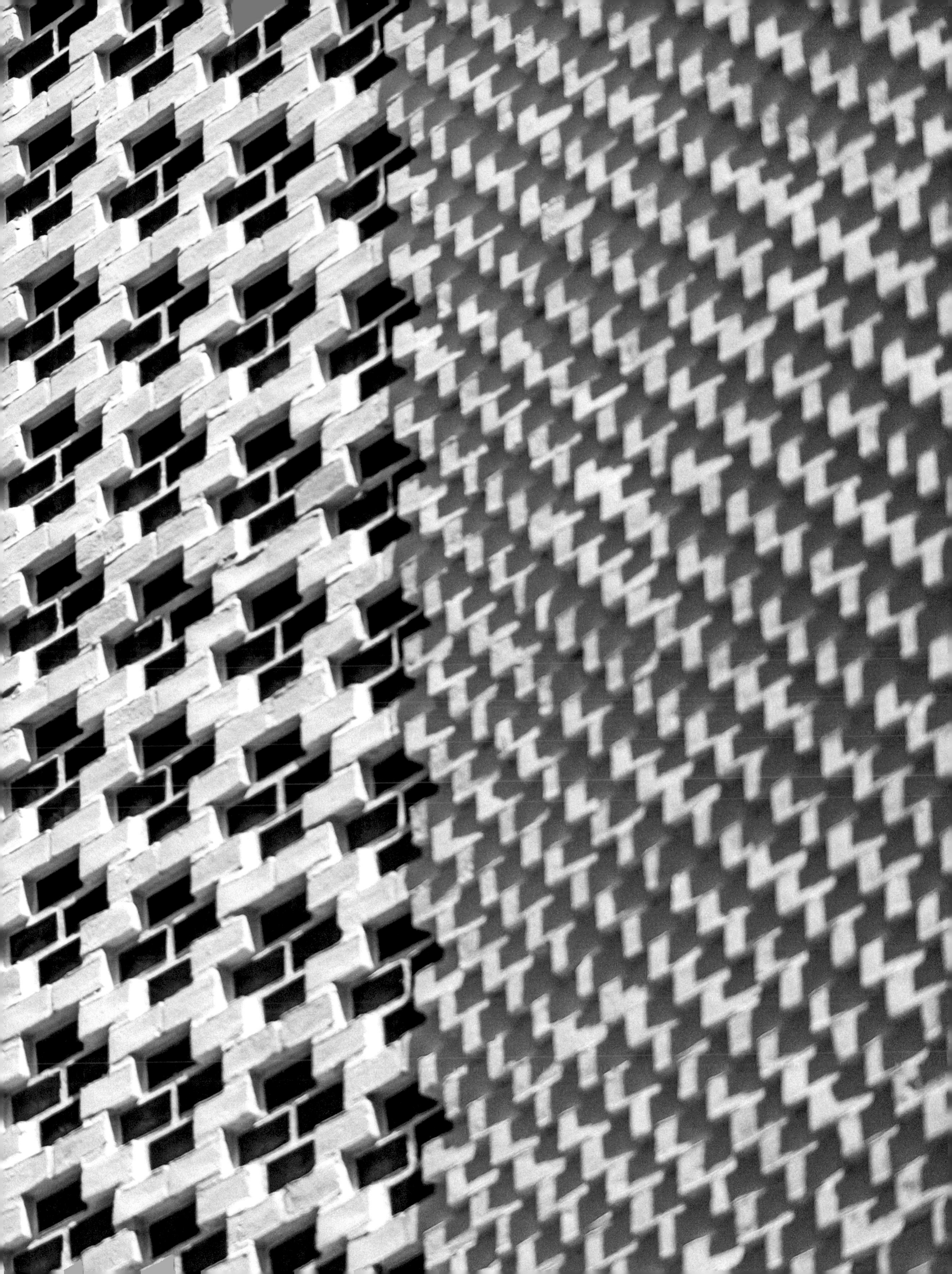